REGENERATION

Stated and Explained According to Scripture and Antiquity with a Summary View of the Doctrine of Justification
(1829)

Regeneration, the process of uniting the inner Godly part of man with the One True God is herein fully explained and developed in this scarce treatise.

Rev. Daniel Waterland

ISBN 1-56459-587-0

SKETCH OF THE AUTHOR.

"Few names," says Dr. Van Mildert, the present learned bishop of Durham, "recorded in the annals of the Church of England, stand so high in the estimation of its most sound and intelligent members as that of Dr. Waterland.—His writings continue to be referred to by divines of the highest character, and carry with them a weight of authority never attached but to names of acknowledged pre-eminence in the learned world."

Dr. Daniel Waterland was the son of the Rev. Henry Waterland, and was born at Walesby, England, February 14th, 1683. His early talents were such, that many of his school exercises were "handed abroad, for the honour of the school" in which he received his education. In his 16th year he entered Magdalen College, Cambridge, of which fourteen years afterward he became master. Soon after he graduated he was admitted to holy orders, and obtained a small living, but continued for many years to devote himself to the work of tuition, giving up almost the whole revenue of his living to his curate, and during this period he pursued those studies, which at length placed him among the most distinguished theologians of his age.

In 1717 he was appointed one of the royal chaplains. In 1719 he published his first work, which brought to him applause as an author. It was a Vindication of Christ's divinity, in opposition to the celebrated Samuel Clarke. The controversy had been sometime commenced, and Dr. Clarke, who had borne a prominent part, had obtained considerable reputation; but from the time that Waterland engaged in it, the reputation and authority of Clarke sensibly declined, while Waterland advanced rapidly in public estimation, and readily removed many of the difficulties which Clarke had thrown in the way of this important doctrine. Dr. Waterland's biographer says of his writings in this controversy, that they "manifested a vigorous understanding, acute discernment, laborious research, a clear conception even of the most intricate points, and a complete mastery of his whole subject."

But the literary labours of Dr. Waterland were not confined to a vindication of the peculiar doctrines of the gospel against heretical writers. The times in which he lived were not destitute of talented enemies to the gospel itself. Against some of these also he took up the polished weapons of his warfare, and with much success to the cause, as well as addition to his reputation.

. His publications were, however, much more numerous and extensive, but it is not the purpose of this sketch, to go into an enumeration of them.

In 1730 he was collated by Bishop Gibson to the archdeaconry of Middlesex, an appointment peculiarly suited to his habits and acquirements, and affording full scope for the exercise of his varied attainments, yet in the midst of incessant avocations he was not averse from habits of social intercourse, but freely cultivated and improved his acquaintance with those around him, and found leisure to assist and encourage others in every laudable undertaking.

He died a little before his entrance upon his fifty-eighth year, and was interred in the chapel royal at Windsor—having for some years stood high in the estimation of men of the first character and station in the English church, and the English universities, at a period when theology and literature might boast in them some of their brightest ornaments.

Bishop Van Mildert, in his review of Dr. Waterland's life and writings, from which this sketch has been drawn, says of his works, that "a vein of genuine piety runs through all his writings, unmixed with party spirit, unostentatious, unassuming, neither lax nor bigoted, neither fanciful nor austere. His style is that of a writer less intent upon the manner, than upon the matter of his productions. He formed distinct conceptions of what he had to deliver, thought deeply yet clearly upon the point to be discussed, and clothed his thoughts in that diction which would best enable the reader to apprehend them with facility. There is also a spirit and vivacity in his writings, which, without any effort to attract, excites attention, and sustains it more effectually than could be done by artificial powers of composition."

Mr. Seed, himself a theologian of some reputation, says of Dr. Waterland's personal character, that "he was a man of cool wisdom and steady piety; fixed in his principles, but candid in his spirit; easy of access, his carriage free and familiar; cautious, but not artful; honest, but not unguarded; glad to communicate, though not ambitious to display his great knowledge. He hated all *party*, as such; and would never have gone the length of any. He was not one of those narrow spirited men, who confine all merit within their own pale: he thought candidly, and spoke advantageously, of many who thought very differently from him. He had nothing violent in his nature: he abhorred all thoughts of persecution: cool and prudential measures entirely suited his frame of mind. Controversy had not at all embittered, or set an edge upon his spirits."

Of the two tracts which follow from his pen, the first, *Regeneration stated and explained*, is the substance of two sermons upon Titus iii. 4, 5, 6. This tract is said to have been peculiarly seasonable at the time it first appeared. Recent controversies render its republication at this time equally so. Nothing can be more simple and intelligible than the explanation of this doctrine here given, or more conformable with the Scriptures and with the articles and formularies of our church. It is believed that no attempts to controvert this statement of the doctrine have ever been made.

The *Summary View of Justification*, which accompanies the above tract, is an attempt to restore the doctrine to its original and scriptural meaning, and this is done by reference to Scripture, reason, and the received opinions of the universal church; and the deviations of modern writers from these high authorities are examined and refuted.

These tracts are text books on their several subjects in the General Theological Seminary of the Protestant Episcopal Church. They are here printed *verbatim* from Van Mildert's edition of his works.

May that Divine Being from " whom all holy desires, all good counsels, and all just works proceed," bless the perusal of these tracts to the accomplishment of his own wise purposes in the souls of all who read them!
EDITOR.

REGENERATION

STATED AND EXPLAINED

ACCORDING TO

SCRIPTURE AND ANTIQUITY,

IN A

DISCOURSE ON TITUS III. 4, 5, 6.

But after that the kindness and love of God our Saviour toward man appeared, not by works of righteousness which we have done, but according to his mercy he saved us, by the washing of regeneration, and renewing of the Holy Ghost; which he shed on us abundantly, through Jesus Christ our Saviour.—*Titus* iii. 4, 5, 6.

Sᴛ. Pᴀᴜʟ in these words has briefly taught us God's method of saving both Jew and Gentile, under the Christian dispensation. He did it, and does it, of free *grace*, and according to the riches of his *pure mercy;* not for or by any righteousness which *we* have done or do by our own *unassisted* abilities,* but by the " washing (or laver) of regeneration, and renewing of the Holy Ghost :" that is to say, by the sacrament of Christian *baptism*, considered in both its *parts*, the *outward* visible *sign*, which is *water*, and the *inward* things *signified* and exhibited, *viz.* a death unto sin, and a new birth unto righteousness, therein wrought by the Holy Spirit of God. I interpret the text of *water-baptism*,

* Si quæras cujusmodi opera a justificatione et salute excludat apostolus, clare hic respondet ipse: α ιτοικοαμιν ημυκ, pronomine ημυκ emphatice addito: quæ fecimus ipsi, h. e. ex propriis viribus. Deinde *operibus* hujusmodi, ex ingenio humano profectis, opponit *gratiam* illam Dei, ex mera sua misericordia in nos per Christum largiter effusam, que *regeneramur* ac *renovamur,* quaque *sola* operibus vere bonis idonei redidimur. Quodque *prioribus* ademerat, *his* concedit operibus: h. e. per hæc, non per illa, nos servatos affirmat. Cum enim dicit Paulus, servari nos *δια ανακαινωσιως πνιυματος αγιου,* intelligit omnes illas virtutes ac bona opera quæ a corde per *Spiritum Sanctum* renovato fluunt. *Bull. Harmon. Apost.* dissert. ii. c. 12. p. 485. edit. Lond. 1721.

as the *ancients* constantly did,* and as the rules of true criticism require. For though some *moderns* have endeavoured to explain away the *outward* part, resolving all into the *inward* part or thing signified, namely, the grace of the spirit; yet with how little reason or success they have attempted it, is well known to the more *judicious*, who have abundantly vindicated the ancient construction.† The latter part of the text is nearly parallel to those words of our Lord; " Except a man be born of water and of the spirit, he cannot enter into the kingdom of heaven."‡ And the general doctrine both of our Lord and St. Paul in those texts, is, that *water* applied outwardly to the body, together with the *grace* of the spirit applied inwardly to the soul, *regenerate* the man:§ or, in other words, the Holy Spirit, in and by the use of water-baptism, causes the *new birth*. But it is observable, that while our Lord's words make mention only of the *new birth*, that is, of *regeneration*, the apostle here in the text distinctly speaks both of a *regeneration* and a *renovation*, as two things, and both of them wrought ordinarily in one and the same *baptism*, here called the laver *of regeneration*, and of *renewing*. Indeed the words of the *original* may be rendered, by the laver *of regeneration*, and *by the renewing;* and so some have translated or interpreted them.‖ But the

---

* *Baptisma* enim esse in quo homo vetus moritur et novus nascitur, manifestat et probat beatus Apostolus dicens: *Servavit nos per lavacrum regenerationis.* Si autem in lavacro, id est, in *baptismo,* est regeneratio, quomodo generare filios Deo hæresis per Christum potest, &c. *Cyprian.* ep. lxxiv. p. 140. edit. Benedict. item epist. i. p. 2. Conf. Origen. in Matt. p. 391. ed. Huet. Theophil. ad Autol. lib. ii. c. 25. p. 153. Chrysostom. ad Illumin. Catech. 1 tom. ii. p. 228. ed. Bened.

† See Whitby on the text. Wolfius, Cur. Crit. in loc.

‡ John iii. 5. That this text also was anciently understood of *water-baptism,* and ought to be so, has been abundantly proved by the best learned moderns, *viz.* Hooker, vol. ii. book v. numb. 59. p. 243. Ox. ed. Maldonate in loc. Lightfoot, tom. i. p. 571, &c. Wall, Infant Baptism, part i. p. 6, 22. part ii. p. 165. Defence, p. 11, 24, 153, 237. Wolfius, Cur. Crit. in loc. vol. i. p. 811, &c. Beveridge's Sermons, vol. iii. serm. xi. p. 319, &c.

§ *Aqua* igitur exhibens forinsecus *sacramentum* gratiæ, et *Spiritus* operans intrinsecus *beneficium* gratiæ, solvens vinculum culpæ, reconcilians bonum naturæ, *regenerant* hominem in uno *Christo,* ex uno *Adamo* generatum. *Augustin. Epist. ad Bonifac.* xcviii. p. 264. edit. Bened. Conf. Origen. in Johann. p. 124, 125. ed. Huet.

‖ Per lavacrum regenerationis, et renovationem Spiritus Sancti. So Jerome in his comment on the place, tom. iv. p. 435. edit. Bened.—

common rendering appears to be preferable, as best warranted by the *reading*, and by the ancient *versions*, and by the general doctrine of the New Testament in relation to *baptism*, as ordinarily carrying with it, in *adults* at least fitly prepared, both a *regeneration* and a *renovation:* which, though distinct in name and notion, (as appears from this text, and from several other texts of the New Testament, to be hereafter mentioned,) are yet nearly allied in end and use; are of one and the same original, often go together, and are perfective of each other. In discoursing farther, my design is,

I. To explain the name and notion of *regeneration*, showing what it is, and what it contains; as also what concern it has with Christian baptism, called the laver, or fountain of it.

II. To consider what the *renewing* mentioned in the text means, and how it differs from or agrees with *regeneration;* and what connexion both have either with *baptism* here, or with *salvation* hereafter.

III. To draw some proper *inferences* from the whole, for preventing mistakes in these high matters, and for our better improvement in Christian knowledge and practice.

I.

First, I propose to treat of *regeneration*, showing what it means, and what it contains, and what relation it bears to Christian baptism, called the *laver*, or fountain of it. *Regeneration*, passively considered, is but another word for the *new birth* of a Christian: and that new birth, in the general, means a spiritual *change* wrought upon any person, by the Holy Spirit, in the use of *baptism;* whereby he is translated from his *natural* state in *Adam*, to a *spiritual* state in *Christ.* The name, or the notion, probably, was not altogether *new* in our Lord's time: for the Jews had been used to admit converts from heathenism into the Jewish Church, by a *baptism* of their own; and they called the admission or reception of such converts by the name of *regeneration* or *new birth;* as it was somewhat like the bringing them into a *new world.* Such *proselytes* were considered as *dead* to their former state of darkness, and born anew to light,

As if *δια* were understood before *αναχαινασιας.* And so some of the critics, in Poole's Synopsis.

liberty, and privileges, among the children of Israel, and within the church of God. The figure was easy, natural, and affecting; and therefore our Lord was pleased, in his conference with Nicodemus, to adopt the same kind of language, applying it to the case of admitting converts both from *Judaism* and *Paganism* into Christianity; transferring and sanctifying the rite, the figure, and the name, to higher and holier, but still *similar* purposes. Such is the account given of this matter by many learned and judicious writers.* It appears extremely probable, from the authorities commonly cited for it; and it is particularly favoured by those words of our Lord to Nicodemus, expressing some kind of marvel at his slowness of apprehension; "Art thou a master of Israel, and knowest not these things?"† Some doubts have been raised on this head, and some very learned persons have expressed their diffidence about it: but, all things considered, there does not appear to be sufficient reason to make question of it.‡ So much for the *name* and *notion* of *regeneration*, and the *original* of it, together with the *occasion* of our Lord's applying it to this case. Indeed, he *improved* the notion, by the addition of the *spirit:* and he *enlarged* the use of the rite, by ordering that *every one*, every convert to Christianity, every candidate for heaven, should be baptized.§ *Every one* must be born *of water and*

* Selden, de Jur. Nat. et Gent. lib. ii. c. 2, 3, 4. Elderfield of Regeneration, Hebrew and Christian. Wall, Infant Baptism, introduct. p. 95, &c. Defence, p. 22, 26, 35, 211, 318. Wotton, Miscellan. Disc. vol. i. p. 103, &c. Vitringa, Observ. Sacr. lib. ii. c. 6. p. 322. Others referred to in Fabricius, Bibl. Antiq. p. 386. Archbishop Sharpe, vol. iii. serm. xiii. p. 280. Deylingius, Observ. Sacr. part. iii. dissert. 34. p. 323, 324. Wesselius, dissert. xv. de Bapt. Proselytorum, p. 444, &c.   † John iii. 10.

‡ The very learned Wolfius several times speaks doubtfully of it, Cur. Critic. vol. i. p. 53, 815. vol. ii. p. 445. But it will be proper to compare Wesselius, who has appeared since, and who has professedly treated this argument, and done it in a very accurate way, recapitulating all that had been urged on both sides the question, and at length deciding in favour of what I have mentioned. The title of the book is, Johannis Wesselii Dissertationes Academicæ, ad selecta quædam loca V. et N. Testamenti. Lugd. Batavorum. A. D. 1734.

§ "What alterations were intended to be made by our Lord, he himself declared: he told Nicodemus, that *except a man* (τις, i. e. *every one*, without distinction of sexes,) *be born again, he cannot enter into the kingdom of God.* He there shows that baptism was instituted for *all mankind*, in opposition to their doctrine who taught that children of

the spirit: not *once* born of water, and *once* of the spirit, so as to make *two* new births,[*] or to be regenerated *again* and *again*, but to be once new born of *both*, once born of the spirit, in or by water; while the spirit primarily or effectively, and the water secondarily or instrumentally, concurs to one and the same birth, ordinarily the result of *both*,[†] in virtue of the divine appointment.

Hence it was, that the ancient doctors of the church, in explaining this article, were wont to consider the *spirit* and the *water* under the lively emblem of a *conjugal* union, as the two *parents;* and the new-born Christian as the *offspring* of both.[‡] The Holy Spirit was understood to *impregnate*, as it were, the waters of the font, (like as he once *overshadowed* the blessed Virgin,) in order to make them conceive and bring forth that *holy thing* formed after Christ; namely, the *new man.* Whatever aptness or justness there may or may not be in the *similitude*, (for *figures* of speech ought not to be strained to a *rigorous* exactness,) yet one thing is certain, that the ancients took *baptism* into their notion of *regeneration.* A learned writer has well proved at large, beyond all reasonable contradiction, that both the Greek and Latin fathers, not only used that word for *baptism*, but so *appropriated* it also to baptism, as to *exclude* any other conversion, or repentance, not considered with *baptism*, from being signified by that name;[§] so that accord-

proselytes, born after *proselytism*, needed not to be baptized." *Wotton, Miscell. Disc.* vol. i. p. 111.

[*] Vid. Marckii Dissertat. Syllog. ad N. Test. dissert. xxi. p. 355, 356.

[†] Neque enim Spiritus sine aqua operari potest, neque aqua sine Spiritu: *Concil. Carthag. apud Cyprian.* p. 330. edit. Bened. conf. p. 148, 149, 260. Cyrill. Catech. iii. p. 41.

Nos pisciculi, secundum 'Ιχθυν nostrum, Jesum Christum, *in aqua nascimur*, nec aliter quam in aqua permanendo salvi sumus. *Tertullian. de Bapt.* c. i. p. 224. Conf. Ger. Voss. Opp. tom. vi. p. 269.

[‡] See my Christian Sacrifice explained, Appendix, vol. viii. p. 188, 189. and Sacramental Part of the Eucharist explained, vol. viii. p. 229. And to the authorities there referred to may be added Theodorus Mopsuestenus, Apollinarius, and Ammonius, cited in Conderius's Greek Catena on John iii. 5. p. 89.

Some considered the *Church* and the *Spirit* as the two parents, as St. Austin often does, and Leo the First, and others: but still the notion was much the same, because the church was supposed to be a parent only in and by the use of *water-baptism.*

[§] Wall, Infant Baptism, part i. xcv. 22, 25, 28, 29, 30. Defence, p.

ing to the ancients, *regeneration*, or *new birth*, was either
baptism itself, (including both *sign* and *thing*,) or a change
of man's spiritual state considered as wrought by the *spirit*
in or through baptism. This new birth, this regeneration,
could be but *once* in a Christian's whole life, as baptism
could be but *once:* and as there could be no *second* baptism,
so there could be no *second* new birth. Regeneration, with
respect to the regenerating agent, means the first *admission*,
and with respect to the *recipient*, it means the *first entrance*,
into the spiritual or Christian life : and there cannot be two
first entrances, or two *admissions*, any more than two spiritual *lives*, or two baptisms. The analogy which this new
spiritual life bears to the *natural*, demonstrates the same
thing.* There are, in all, *three* several *lives* belonging to
every good Christian, and *three births*, of course, thereto corresponding.† *Once* he is born into the *natural* life, born of
Adam ; *once* he is born into the *spiritual* life, born of *water*
and the *spirit;* and *once* also into a *life* of *glory*, born of the
resurrection at the last day. I mention that *third* birth, into
a life above, because that birth also seems to have the name
of *regeneration*, in the New Testament.‡ But my present
concern is only with the *regeneration* proper to this life,
which comes but *once*, and admits not of a *second*, during
this mortal state.§ This *regeneration*, in the *active* sense,

12, 34, 41, 277, 318, 323, 327, 329, 333, 343. Append. p. 4, 6.
Comp. Archbishop Sharpe, vol. iii. serm. xiii. p. 280, &c. Suicer.
Thesaur. tom. i. p. 243, 396, 639, 1352. tom. ii. p. 278, 549, 554.
Cangius, Glossar. Græc. p. 1084. Bingham, xi. 1, 3. p. 462.

* Cum ergo sint duæ nativitates——una est de terra, alia de cœlo;
una est de carne, alia de spiritu; una est de mortalitate, alia de æter-
nitate; una est de masculo et fœmina, alia de Deo et Ecclesia. Sed
ipsæ duæ *singulæ* sunt; nec illa potest *repeti*, nec illa.——Jam natus
sum de *Adam*, non me potest *iterum* generare Adam: jam natus sum
de *Christo*, non me potest *iterum* generare Christus. Quomodo uterus
non potest repeti, sic nec Baptismus. *Augustin. in Johan.* tract. xi.
p. 378. tom. iii. par. 2. edit. Bened. Conf. Prosper. Sentent. 331. p.
246. apud Augustin. tom. x. in Append. Aquinas Summ. par. iii. qu.
66. art. 9. p. 150.

† Vid. Gregor. Nazianz. Orat. xl. p. 637. Origen. in Matt. Orat. ix.
fol. 23. Lat. ed. p. 391. ed. Huet. Augustin. contr. Julian. lib. ii. p.
540, 541.

‡ Matt. xix. 28. See Commentators, and Bishop Pearson on the
Creed, art. i. p. 28. and particularly Olearius in Matt. p. 540.

§ Ουκ ευσης δευτερας αναγιννησιης, ουδι αναπλασιας, κ. τ. λ. *Nazianz.*
Orat. xl. p. 641. Conf. Nicet. Serron. Comment. p. 1048. Semel per-

is what St. Peter speaks of, where he says, "God hath begotten us again unto a lively hope."[*] And afterwards, in the same chapter, but in the *passive* sense, " Being born again, not of corruptible seed, but incorruptible, by the word of God :"[†] that is, by the *words* used in the *form* of *baptism;* or else by the *word* preached, conducting men to *faith* and *baptism.* These texts relating to the *new birth,* speak of it as a *transient* thing, once performed, and retaining its *virtue* during the whole spiritual life. But when the phrase of *born of God* is found to denote a *permanent state,*[‡] it is to be understood of a person who *has been* born of God, and *abides* entirely in that *sonship,* that spiritual and salutary state which he was *once* born into: so the phrase, *born of a woman,* is often used as equivalent to *son of a woman,* by a figure of speech,[§] and is easily understood. *Regeneration,* on the part of the *grantor,* God Almighty, means *admission* or *adoption*‖ into sonship, or spiritual citizenship: and on the part of the *grantee,* viz. man, it means his *birth,* or entrance into that state of sonship, or citizenship. It is God that *adopts* or *regenerates,* like as it is God that *justifies.*[¶] Man does not *adopt, regenerate,* or *justify* himself, whatever hand he may otherwise have (but still under *grace*) in *preparing* or *qualifying* himself for it. God makes the *grant,* and it is entirely *his act:* man *receives* only, and is acted upon ; though sometimes *active* in qualifying himself, as in the case of *adults,* and sometimes entirely *passive,* as in the case of *infants.* The thing granted and received is a change from the state natural into the state spiritual ; a translation from the *curse of Adam* into the *grace of Christ.* This *change, translation,* or *adoption,* carries in it many Christian blessings and privileges, but all reducible to two, *viz. remission of sins,* (absolute or condi-

ceptam parvulus gratiam non amittit nisi propria impietate, si ætatis accessu tam malus evaserit. Tunc enim etiam propria incipiet habere peccata; quæ non *regeneratione* auferantur, sed *alia* curatione sanentur. *Augustin. ad Bonifac.* tom. ii. ep. 98. p. 264. ed. Bened. Conf. Damascen ad Hebr. vi. 6. Opp. tom. ii. p. 237. ed. sequ.

[*] 1 Peter i. 3.   [†] 1 Peter i. 23.   [‡] 1 John iii. 9. iv. 7. v. 1, 4, 18.
[§] Job xiv. 1. xv. 14. xxv. 4. Matth. xi. 11. Luke vii. 28.
‖ Rom. viii. 15. Gal. iv. 5. Ephes. i. 5. John i. 12. Note, that our *adoptive* sonship is opposed to our Lord's *natural* sonship, the foundation of our *adoption.*
[¶] Vid. Bull's Harmon. Apóst. par, ii. ç. 2. p. 418.

tional,) and a *covenant claim*, for the time being, *to eternal happiness.* Those blessings may all be forfeited, or finally lost, if a person revolts from God, either for a time or for ever; and then such person is no longer in a *regenerate* state, or a state of *sonship*, with respect to any *saving* effects: but still God's original grant of adoption or sonship in baptism stands in full force, to take place as often as any such revolter shall return, and not otherwise: and if he desires to be as before, he will not want to be *regenerated* again, but renewed, or reformed. *Regeneration complete* stands in two things, which are, as it were, its two *integral* parts, the *grant* made over to the person, and the *reception* of that grant. The grant once made, *continues* always the same: but the reception may *vary*, because it depends upon the condition of the recipient.*

II.

Having said what I conceived sufficient upon the first article, respecting *regeneration*, I now proceed to the second, which is *renovation;* and which I understand of a *renewal* of *heart*, or *mind*. Indeed, *regeneration* is itself a kind of *renewal;* but then it is of the *spiritual state*, considered *at large;* whereas *renovation*, the other article in the text, seems to mean a more *particular* kind of *renewal*, namely, of the inward *frame*, or *disposition* of the man: which is rather a *capacity*, or *qualification*, (in *adults*,) for *salutary* regeneration, than the regeneration itself. *Regeneration* may be granted and received (as in *infants*) where that *renovation* has no place at all, for the time being: and therefore, most certainly, the notions are very distinct. But of this I may say more hereafter in a proper place. It may here be further noted, that *renovation* may be, and should be, with respect to adults, *before*, and *in*, and *after* baptism. *Preventing* grace must go before, to work in the man *faith* and *repentance*, which are qualifications previous to baptism, and necessary to render it *salutary*. Those first addresses, or influential visits, of the Holy Spirit, turning and preparing the heart of man, are the preparative *renewings*, the first and lowest degrees of *renovation.*† Afterwards, in baptism, the

* "As many as received him, to them gave he power to become the sons of God." John i. 12. Rom. viii. 14, 15.

† *Spiramen* est modicæ virtutis aliqua gratia, in audienda lege Dei

same spirit fixes, as it were, his *dwelling*, or residential *abode*, renewing the heart in *greater* measure :* and if his motions are still more and more complied with after baptismal regeneration, the *renewing* grows and improves through the whole course of the spiritual life.† Therefore, though we find no Scripture exhortations made to *Christians* (for Nicodemus was a *Jew*,) to become *regenerated*, yet we meet with several exhortations to them to be again and again *renewed*. For example: " Be ye transformed by the renewing of your mind ;"‡ " Be renewed in the spirit of your minds."§ The " inward man" is said to be " renewed day by day."|| And when Christians have once fallen off, the *restoring* them again is not called *regenerating* them, but " renewing them again unto repentance."¶ Of this *renovation* of the heart, we may best understand the phrase of " putting on the new man,"** amounting to much the

multorum *primum: Spiritus* autem, perfectionis est *plenitudo. Spiramen* itaque datur ab infantia et *catechumenis: Spiritus* autem in incremento *doctrinæ fideique*, et salutaris *Baptismi* plena Dei gratia, ut intelligere, et ad majorem jam possit scientiam pervenire. *Philastr. contr. Hær.* n. 147. p. 329. ed. Fabric.

* *Spiritus ubi vult spirat;* sed quod fatendum est, aliter adjuvat *nondum inhabitans*, aliter *inhabitans:* nam nondum inhabitans adjuvat *ut sint fideles*, inhabitans adjuvat *jam fideles*. *Augustin ad Xyst.* ep. 194. p. 720.

In quibusdam tanta est *gratia* fidei quanta non sufficit ad obtinendum regnum cœlorum: sicut in *catechumenis*, sicut in ipso Cornelio antequam *sacramentorum* participatione *incorporaretur* Ecclesiæ: in quibusdam vero tanta est ut jam *corpori* Christi, et sancto Dei *templo* deputentur. *Augustin de Divers. Q. ad simplicium*, tom. vi. lib. 1. p. 89. ed. Bened.

† Hæc *Spiritus donatio*, quæ *justificationem* sequitur, a *gratia* ejusdem Spiritus hominis conversionem *prævcniente* et operante bifariam imprimis differt. Primo, Quod animæ jam a vitiis purgatæ Spiritus divinus *arctius* atque *intimius* quam antea *unitur*, in ipsam altius penetrat, pleniusque ejus facultates omnes pervadit. Unde in Scripturis dicitur Spiritus divinus ante *conversionem* hominis, quasi *ad cordis ostium pulsare*, post conversionem vero *interiora* domus *intrare. Apoc.* iii. 20. Deinde, quod sanctissimus ille Spiritus in anima, quam antea veluti *inviserat* tantum, et gratia sua *prævcniente* in domicilium sibi *præparaverat*, jam *habitat* et quasi *sedem* suam *figit;* nunquam inde discessurus, nisi per peccatum aliquod gravius foras extrudatur. *Bull. Apolog. contra Tulliun*, p. 15. alias p. 643.

‡ Rom. xii. 2.

§ Ephes. iv. 23. or, *by the spirit of your mind.* See Bishop Bull's Posth. p. 1135, 1136. || 2 Cor. iv. 16. ¶ Hebr. vi. 6.

** Ephes. iv. 24. Coloss. iii. 10.

same with "having on the breast-plate of righteousness ;"*
and "putting on the armour of light,"† and "putting on
bowels of mercies," with other Christian virtues or graces.‡
Of the same import is the phrase of *putting on Christ;* plainly in one of the places,§ and probably in the other also :‖
though some interpret the former of *renovation*, and the latter of *regeneration*.¶   Lastly, the phrase of *new creature***
may properly be referred to *renovation* also, and is so interpreted by the *ancients*†† generally: or if it be referred to
regeneration, as ordinarily including and comprehending
renovation under it, that larger construction of it will not
perhaps be amiss.

The *distinction*, which I have hitherto insisted upon, between *regeneration* and *renovation*, has been carefully kept
up by the Lutheran divines especially,‡‡ as of great use.
And it is what our church appears to have gone upon, in
her *offices* of baptism, as likewise in the catechism. She
clearly expresses it in one of her collects, wherein we beg
of God, that we being *regenerate* and made his children by
adoption and grace, may daily be *renewed* by his Holy Spirit, &c.:§§ such is the *public* voice of our church. What
the *private* sentiments of some divines have been, or how
far they have overlooked, or not attended to, this so necessary distinction, is not material to inquire: but that it never
has been lost amongst us may appear from the words of a
very judicious divine of this present age.‖‖ The difference
between these two may be competently understood from
what has been already said: but to make it still clearer, it
may be drawn out more minutely, in distinct articles, as

---

* Ephes. vi. 14. 1 Thes. v. 8.   † Rom. xiii. 12.   •
‡ Coloss. iii. 12.   § Rom. xiii. 14. See Whitby and Wolfius in loc.
‖ Gal. iii. 27. Vid. Wolfius in loc.
¶ Deylingius, Observ. Sacr. tom. iii. dissert. 42. p. 406.
** 2 Cor. v. 17. Gal. vi. 15. See Whitby and Wolfius; and Bishop
Beveridge, vol. ii. serm. vii.
†† See the passages collected in Suicer, tom. ii. p. 178, 179.
‡‡ Vid. Gerhard, Loc. Comm. tom. iv. p. 495, 503, &c. conf. tom.
iii. p. 713, &c.   §§ Collect for Christmas-day.
‖‖ "There is a mighty difference between *regeneration* and *renova-
tion:* we can be *born* but *once*, because we can *live* but *once;* and therefore baptism, which gives life, cannot be *repeated:* but we can recover
often, and grow and be nourished *often*, because we can sink and droop
often." *Dean Stanhope, Boyle's Lect.* serm. viii. p. 249. Compare
Archbishop Sharpe, vol. iii. serm. xiii. p. 279.

follows. 1. *Regeneration* and *renovation* differ in respect to the *effective* cause or agency: for one is the work of the *spirit* in the use of *water;* that is, of the spirit *singly*, since *water* really *does* nothing, is no *agent* at all; but the other is the work of the *spirit* and the *man* together. Man *renews* himself at the same time that the spirit *renews* him: and the *renovation* wrought is the result of their *joint agency;* man concurring and operating in a *subordinate* way. "It is God that worketh in us both to will and to do:"* but still it is supposed, and said, that we both *will* and *do*. It is God that *renews, cleanses,* and *purifies* the heart:† and man also renews, cleanses, and purifies his own heart;‡ that is, he bears his part in it, be it more or less. No man *regenerates* himself at all; that is, he has no part in the *regenerating act,* (which is entirely God's,) whatever he may have in the *receptive:* and if in this sense only it be said, that man is purely *passive* in it, it is true and sound doctrine. Nevertheless, he may and must be *active* in preparing and qualifying himself for it, and in receiving it, supposing him to be *adult*. He is not his own *regenerator,* or *parent,* at all, in his new birth: for that would be a *solecism* in speech, and a contradiction in notion: he is, however, his own *renewer,* though in part only, and in subordination to the *principal* agent. 2. Another difference between *regeneration* and *renovation* (before hinted) is, that *regeneration* ordinarily is in or through *baptism* only, a transient thing, which comes but once:§ whereas *renovation* is before, and

* Phil. ii. 13.   † Psal. xix. 12. li. 2, 10. Jer. xxiv. 7. Ezek. xi. 19. xxxvi. 26. Acts xv. 9. Tit. iii. 5. 1 John i. 9.

‡ Psalm cxix. 9. lxxiii. 13. Isa. i. 16. Ezek. xviii. 31. 2 Cor. vii. 1. James iv. 8. 1 Peter i. 22. 1 John iii. 3. Conf. Cyrill. Hierosol. Catech. i. p. 16, 17. ed. Bened.

§ The late learned Regius Professor of Divinity, at Cambridge, Dr. Beaumont, in his MS. Commentary on Rom. xii. 2. writes thus:

Sed scrupulum hic injicies: nonne enim Apostolus commonefacit fratres suos, adeoque Christianos, per Baptismum *regenitos,* adeoque et αναχχαιωσιν istam adeptos? Quid opus igitur actum agere? Nil sane. Nec monet eos baptisma iterare: *semel nascimur, renascimur semel:* unus Dominus, una fides, unum baptisma, Ephes. iv. 5. Quoniam vero ipsi *renati* ex baptismali puritate non raro relabuntur ad *veteris hominis* inquinamenta, ex usu eorum est assidua per pœnitentiam *renovatio.* Hinc Chrysostomus, &c. Then he quotes Chrysostom's words on Rom. xii. 2. Hom. xx. p. 659. tom. ix. ed. Bened. and afterwards adds, Similia videas apud Photium et Theophylactum.

in, and after baptism, and may be often repeated : continuing and increasing from the first *preparations* to Christianity, through the whole progress of the Christian life. So it is in *adults :* but in *infants,* regeneration commences *before* renovation; which again shows how distinct and different they are. 3. A third observable difference is, that *regeneration* once given can never be *totally* lost, any more than *baptism;* and so can never want to be *repeated* in the *whole* thing; whereas *renovation* may be often *repeated,* or may be totally lost. *Once regenerate and always regenerate,* in some part, is a true maxim in Christianity, only not in such a sense as some *moderns* have taught.* But a person once *regenerated* in baptism can never want to be regenerated again in this life, any more than he can want to be *rebaptized.* So much for the *difference* between *regeneration* and *renovation :†* let us next consider how far they *agree,* or how near they are *allied.* As one is a renewal of the *spiritual state,* and the other a renewal of the *heart* and *mind,* it must follow, that so far as a renewal of *mind* is necessary to a renewal of *state,* so far it is a necessary ingredient of the *new birth,* or an *integral part* of it. A grant is suspended,

---

* Those I mean who have taught that the *regenerate* can never *finally* fall from *grace.* See our Sixteenth Article on this head.

† Vossius distinguishes *regeneration* from *renovation* by what they respectively *contain,* thus:

Quemadmodum vero ad *regenerationem,* pressius sumptam, pertinet *remissio* peccatorum; ita ad *renovationem* refertur *mortificatio* veteris, et *vivificatio* novi hominis: quæ idcirco *Baptismo* tribuuntur. *Voss. de Bapt.* Disp. ix. Thes. 6. Opp. tom. vi. p. 270. Gerhard distinguishes nearly the same way in his Common-Places, tom. iii. p. 714. tom. iv. p. 495, 504.

Regenerationis vocabulum quandoque *generale* est, ipsam quoque *renovationem* in ambitu suo complectens: interim tamen, proprie et accurate loquendo, *regeneratio* a *renovatione* distincta est. Tom. iv. p. 495. Renovatio, licet a *regeneratione* proprie et specialiter accepta distinguatur, induo tamen et perpetuo nexu cum ea est conjuncta ——Per Baptismum homo non solum *renascitur,* (id est, peccatorum *remissionem* consequitur, *justitiam Christi* induit, *filius* Dei, et *hæres* vitæ æternæ efficitur,) sed etiam *renovatur:* hoc est, datur ipsi Spiritus Sanctus, qui *intellectum, voluntatem,* et omnes *animi* vires *renovare* incipit, ut amissa *Dei imago* in ipso incipiat *instaurari,* &c. p. 504. *Regenerationis* vox quandoque sumitur γενικως, ut et *remissionem* peccatorum, et *renovationem* simul complectatur; quandoque vero ιδικως accipitur, ut *remissionem* peccatorum ac gratuitam *justificationem* tantummodo designat. *Gerhard,* tom. iii. p. 714.

frustrate, as to any *beneficial* effect, while not properly received : and while there is an insuperable bar to the salutary reception of it, it cannot be savingly *received* or *applied.* Therefore in the case of *adults*, regeneration and renovation must go together : otherwise the regeneration is not a *salutary* nor a complete *regeneration*, wanting one necessary ingredient of it, namely, a *capacity* or *qualification.*

But this may still be more clearly understood by applying those *general* principles to four *special* cases, which I shall next endeavour to do, and then shall take leave of this head. The *four* cases are: 1. The case of *grown* persons coming to baptism in their *integrity*, and so continuing afterwards. 2. The case of *infants* brought in their *innocency*, and leading the rest of their lives according to that beginning. 3. The case of such grown persons or infants so baptized, but *falling off* afterwards. 4. The case of grown persons coming to baptism in *hypocrisy* or *impenitency*; but repenting afterwards and turning to God. The considering how the affair of *regeneration* or *renovation* may respectively stand in each of these cases, may perhaps serve to clear up the whole matter to greater satisfaction.

1. I begin with the case of *grown* persons, called *adults,* coming to baptism fitly prepared by faith and repentance, and afterwards persevering to the end. This was a common case in the earliest days of Christianity, when the whole world wanted to be converted. *Grown* persons were then the most, and the most considerable candidates for baptism. When the discipline of the church came to be settled into something of a regular and standing form, those candidates for baptism were trained up beforehand, by proper instructions, and were therefore called *catechumens.** Afterwards they were to be admitted to *baptism*, when fitly prepared, in order to be effectually " born of water and the spirit," and so made living members of Christ, children of God, and heirs of the kingdom of heaven. *Faith* and *repentance* alone, though both of them were antecedently *gifts* of the *spirit*, were not supposed *ordinarily* to make them *regenerate*, or to entitle them to *salvation*, without *baptism*, by the Scripture accounts.† There might be some special

* Bingham, x. 1, 4.

† Mark xvi. 16. John iii. 5. Ephes. v. 26. 1 Cor. xii. 13. 1 Pet. iii. 21.

cases, or uncommon circumstances, where *martyrdom* supplied the place of *water-baptism*, or where *extremities* were supposed to *supersede* it ;* in which cases inward regeneration might be perfected without the outward *sign* and *sacrament* of it : but, according to the *ordinary* rule, faith and repentance were to be perfected by *baptism*, both for the making *regeneration* and the giving a title to *salvation*.† For without baptism a person is not *regenerate;* at least, not in the eye of the church, which must judge by the *ordinary* rule, and which cannot *dispense*, whatever God himself may please to do in such cases.‡ Till baptism succeeds, the solemn and saving *stipulation*§ between God and the party does not pass in due form ; nor the awful *consecration* of the man to Father, Son, and Holy Ghost.|| He is not yet *buried* with Christ *into death*, nor *planted* in the likeness of his *resurrection;*¶ nor indeed *clothed* with Christ, the baptismal garment.** Therefore, in strictness, he is not a *member* of Christ, nor a *child* of God, nor a *citizen* of Christ's kingdom ; but an *alien* still, having no *covenant* claim to the gospel privileges.†† But when a penitent be-

* Bingham, x. ii. 19, 20, 21. p. 42, &c. alias p. 431.   Augustin de Bapt. lib. iv. cap. 22.   Hooker, vol. ii. b. v. n. 60. p. 245. Ox. edit.

† Nisi quis *nascitur ex aqua et Spiritu*, non ibit in regnum Dei: id est, non erit *sanctus*. Ita omnis anima eo usque in *Adam* censetur, donec in *Christo* recenseatur; tam diu *immunda* quamdiu recenseatur: peccatrix autem quia immunda, recipiens ignominiam ex *carnis* societate. *Tertull. de Anima*, cap. xl. p. 294.

'Αρχη μοι ζωης το Βαπτισμα, και πρωτη ημεραν εκεινη η της παλιγγενεσιας ημερα. *Basil. de Spirit. Sanct.* cap. x. p. 22. tom. 3. ed. Bened. Conf. cap. xii. p. 23, 24.   Item Bull. Apolog. p. 650. alias 23.   Damascen. de Rect. Fid. lib. iv. cap. 9. p. 261.   Vossius de Bapt. Opp. tom. vi. p. 269.

‡ Institutio sacramentorum, quantum ad *Deum* autorem, *dispensationis* est; quantum vero ad *hominem* obedientem, *necessitatis:* quoniam in potestate Dei est *præter ista* hominem salvare; sed in potestate hominis non est *sine istis* ad salutem pervenire. *Hugo de Sacrament*. lib. i. cap. 5. in Hooker, vol. ii. p. 249. Ox. edit.

§ See 1 Pet. iii. 22. || Matt. xxviii. 19.

¶ Rom. vi. 3, 4, &c.   ** Gal. iii. 27.

†† As we are not naturally *men* without *birth*, so neither are we *Christian men*, in the eye of the church of God, but by *new birth;* nor, according to the manifest ordinary course of divine dispensation, *new born*, but by that *baptism* which both *declareth* and *maketh* us Christians. In which respect, we justly hold it to be the *door* of our *actual entrance* into God's house, the first apparent beginning of life, a seal perhaps to the *grace* of *election* before received; but to our *sanctifica-*

comes *baptized*, then commences his *new birth*, his *death unto sin*, in the plenary remission of it, (by the *application* of the merits of Christ's death,) and his new *life unto God*, through Jesus Christ once raised from the grave, and from thenceforth ever *living unto God*.* And now that *renovation* which in some degree was *previous* to regeneration, becomes, in greater degrees, a *fruit* and *complement* of it; and it *grows* more and more by the *indwelling* of that same *spirit*, whose remote addresses and distant overtures first brought the man to that *faith* and *repentance*, which prepared him for salutary baptism, and for true and complete sonship, or Christian adoption. More need not be said of the first of the *four* cases, and therefore now I proceed to a second.

2. The second is the case of *infants*. Their innocence and incapacity are to them instead of *repentance*, which they do not need, and of actual *faith*, which they cannot have. They are capable of being savingly *born of water* and the *spirit*, and of being *adopted* into *sonship* with what depends thereupon; because, though they bring no *virtues* with them, no *positive* righteousness, yet they bring no *obstacle* or *impediment*. They *stipulate*, they enter into *contract*, by their sureties, upon a presumptive and interpretative consent: they become *consecrated* in solemn form to *Father, Son*, and *Holy Ghost*: pardon, mercy, and other *covenant privileges*, are made over to them ;† and the Holy Spirit translates them out of their state of *nature* (to which a *curse* belongs) to a state of *grace, favour*, and *blessing*: this is their regeneration.‡ Wherefore in our public offices, formed upon the ancient rules and precedents, we pray, that the infants brought to be baptized may be " washed and sanctified with the Holy Ghost,"—may receive remission of their sins by spiritual

tion here, a step that hath not any before it. *Hooker*, vol. ii. b. 5. n. 60. p. 249. Ox. edit.

* Rom. vi. 10, 11. Mark xvi. 16. Acts viii. 37. x. 47.

† Certe nemo neget, infantes capaces esse beneficii αφεσιν των αμαρτιων, quod δικαιωσιν, *justificationem*, appellare solemus: est enim id beneficium *externum* et σχετικον, quod in infantes ad *Christi Jesu* intercessionem propter ejus υπακοην, *Spiritu Sancto* pro illorum *conversione* et *renovatione*, spondente (liceat hic humano more balbutire) conferri potest. *Vitringa, Obs. Sacr.* lib. ii. cap. 6. p. 338.

‡ Omnes enim venit [Dominus] per semetipsum salvare; omnes, inquam, qui per eum *renascuntur* in Deum; *infantes*, et parvulos, et pueros, et juniores, et seniores. *Iren.* lib. ii. cap. 22. p. 147. ed. Bened. Conf. Voss. tom. vi. p. 278, 307.

regeneration,—may be "born again," and that "the old Adam may be so buried, that the new man may be raised up in them." We declare afterwards, that they are regenerate, and grafted into the body of Christ's church;" giving thanks also to God, that " it hath pleased him to regenerate them with his Holy Spirit, and to receive them for his own children by adoption, and to incorporate them into his holy church."* It may reasonably be presumed, that from the time of their *new birth* of water and the spirit, (which at that very moment is a renewal of their *state* to God-ward,) the renewing also of the *heart* may come gradually on with their first dawnings of *reason*, in such measures as they shall yet be capable of; in a way to us imperceptible, but known to that divine spirit who *regenerates* them, and whose *temple* from thenceforth they are,† till they defile themselves with *actual* and *grievous* sin. In this case, it is to be noted, that regeneration *precedes*, and renovation can only *follow* after:‡ though infants may perhaps be found capable of receiving some seeds of *internal grace* sooner than is commonly imagined.§ But enough of this.

3. A third case which I promised to speak to, is, that of those who fall off after they have once been savingly *regenerated*. If such persons *fall away*, by desertion and disobedience, still their baptismal *consecration*, and their *covenant state* consequent, abide and stand; but without their *saving* effect for the time being: because, without present *renovation*, the *new birth*, or *spiritual life*, as to salutary purposes, is, in a manner, sinking, drooping, ceasing. Their regene-

---

* Public baptism of infants. Compare office of private baptism, where it is said, that the infant *is now by the laver of regeneration in baptism, received into the number of the children of God:* and the catechism, Q. the second, with the answer: and the latter part concerning the sacrament of *baptism.* Compare also the office of confirmation, repeating the same doctrine.

† Vid. Augustin. Epist. clxxxvii. cap. 8. p. 686.

‡ In baptizatis infantibus *præcedit* regenerationis sacramentum, et si Christianam tenuerint pietatem, *sequetur* in corde *conversio,* cujus mysterium præcessit in corpore.——In infantibus qui baptizati *moriuntur,* eadem gratia omnipotentis implere credenda est; quod non ex impia voluntate, sed ex ætatis indigentia, nec *corde credere ad justitiam* possunt, nec *ore confiteri* ad salutem. *Augustin. de Bapt.* lib. v. cap. 24. p. 140. Conf. Nazianz. Orat. xxxvii. p. 609.

§ Vid. Vitringa, Observ. Sacr. lib. ii. cap. 6. p. 329. alias 359. Vossius de Bapt. Disp. vi. Opp. tom. vi. p. 278.

rate state, upon their revolt, is no longer such, in the *full* saving sense, wanting one of its *integral* parts; like as a ruinated house ceases to be an *house*, when it has nothing left but *walls*. But yet as a house, while there are *walls* left, does not need to be *rebuilt* from the ground, but *repaired* only, in order to become a *house* again as before; so a person once savingly *regenerated*, and afterwards losing all the *salutary* use of it, will not want to be *regenerated* again, or *born anew*, but to be *reformed* only. Which when done, his regeneration before decayed, and as to any *saving* effect, for the time well-nigh ruinated, but never *totally* lost,* becomes again *whole* and *entire*. To be short, *perfect* regeneration is to the *spiritual* life what *perfect* health is to the natural: and the *recoveries* of the spiritual *health*, time after time, are not a *new* regeneration, but a restoring or improving of the *old*. To be *born anew*, would be the same thing as to have *all* done over again that God had before done to make a man a Christian, and to put him into a *covenant state:* but since he who is once a Christian is always a Christian, and there is no such thing as a *second* baptism, it is plain that there can be no such thing here as a second *new birth*, or a second *regeneration*. But of this I said enough before.

4. The *fourth* case, which yet remains to be considered, is the case of those who receive baptism (like Simon Magus suppose,) in *hypocrisy* or *impenitency*. Do they therein receive any thing of the Lord? Or if they do, what is it? Are they thereby regenerated, or born again, born of *water* and of the *spirit?* I answer, they are either born of *both*, or of *neither:* for otherwise, "born of water and of the spirit," would not mean *one birth*, but *two;* and so a person might happen to have *two* new births, one of *water* first, and another of the *spirit* afterwards; which cannot reasonably be supposed. Besides that, the being born of *water* only, which really does nothing of itself, could amount only to a *wash-*

---

* Regenerationis gratiam ita etiam hi non minuunt qui dona *non servant*, sicut *lucis* nitorem loca *immunda* non polluunt. Qui ergo gaudes Baptismi perceptione, vive in *novi hominis* sanctitate; et tenens fidem quæ per dilectionem operatur, habe bonum quod nondum habes, ut *prosit* tibi bonum quod habes. *Prosper. Sentent.* 325. *apud Augustin,* tom. x. p. 245. Append.

Spiritalis enim virtus sacramenti ita est ut *lux*, et ab illuminandis *pura* accipitur, et si per *immundos* transeat, non inquinatur. *Augustin. in Johan.* Tract. v. n. 15. p. 327. tom. iii. part. 2.

ing, (nothing better than *being born* of the *flesh,*) and therefore could not be true or valid *baptism* in Christian account.
Shall we then say, that the ungodly and impenitent are in
baptism *born* of the *spirit?* That is a point, which, I apprehend, can neither be affirmed nor denied *absolutely,* but with
proper *distinctions.* It was anciently a kind of maxim or
ruled case in the church, that all *true* and *valid* baptism
must be so made by the *spirit.** And though some seem to
have denied it, or to have demurred upon it,† yet they really
admitted the same thing in other words, by admitting that
all *true* baptism was *Christ's* baptism, and carried a *sanctity*
with it :‡ therefore that part of the dispute was only about

---

* That was a maxim among the Cyprianists especially, (see above,
p. 8.) and so it came down to Jerome, who is very express on that
head.

Apparet Baptisma non esse sine *Spiritu Sancto.*——Illud nobis mon-
straretur, *rerum* esse Baptisma quo *Spiritus Sanctus* adveniat.——
Ecclesiæ Baptisma sine *Spiritu Sancto* nullum est.——Cum Baptisma
Christi sine *Spiritu Sancto* nullum sit.——*Spiritum Sanctum,* quem
nos asserimus in *vero Baptismate* tribui. *Hieron. adv. Lucif.* p. 293,
294, 295. tom. iv. ed. Bened. Conf. Epist. lxxxii. ad Oceanum, p. 651.
tom. iv.

† St Austin was one of those; he writes thus: *Spiritus Sanctus,* dis-
ciplinæ fugiet fictum, nec tamen eum fugiet *Baptismus.*——Potest
Baptisma esse et unde *se aufert* Spiritus Sanctus.——*Induunt* autem
homines Christum, aliquando usque ad *Sacramenti* perceptionem, aliquando et usque ad *ritæ sanctificationem.*——Si Baptisma esse *sine
Spiritu non potest,* habent et spiritum hæretici, sed ad *perniciem,* non
ad *salutem:* sicut habuit Saul, 1 Reg. xviii. 10.——Sicut habent *avari,*
qui tamen non sunt *templum* Dei.——Si autem non habent avari *Spiritum* Dei, et tamen habent Baptisma, potest esse *sine Spiritu* Baptisma. *Augustin. de Bapt.* lib. v. cap. 23, 24. p. 157. tom. ix.

‡ Baptismus Christi, verbis evangelicis *consecratus,* et per adulteros,
et in adulteris *sanctus est,* quamvis illi sint impudici et immundi: quia
ipsa ejus *sanctitas* pollui non potest, et *sacramento* suo *divina* virtus
adsistit, sive ad *salutem* bene utentium, sive ad *perniciem* male utentium. *Augustin. de Bapt.* lib. iii. cap. 10. p. 113. tom. ix. Conf. p.
115, 176, 199, 268, 296. et contr. Epist. Parmen. lib. ii. cap. 13. p.
44, 45, 80. tom. ix.

N. B. As St. Austin allows that *sanctity* goes along with all *true* and
valid baptism, and as all *sanctification* is of and from the *Holy Spirit,*
he must of consequence admit all that Jerome contended for; namely,
that all *valid* baptism is so made by the *Spirit.* Only, he denied such
valid baptism in ill men to be *saving* for the time being: and Jerome
also denied the same; both agreeing that baptism might be *true* and
valid as sanctified by the *Spirit,* though not *salutary* to some persons
in such and such circumstances.

words, both sides agreeing in the main things. The real and full truth of the case I take to lie in the particulars here following. 1. It is certain in the general, that the *Holy Spirit*, some way or other, has a hand in every *true* and *valid* baptism: God never fails as to his part in an awful *sacrament*, however men may guiltily fail in theirs. 2. The *Holy Spirit* is in some sort *offered* to all that receive Christian baptism: for the very nature of a *sacrament* requires that the *sign* and the *grace* should so far go together: and the *unworthy* could not be guilty of *rejecting* the grace while they receive the sign, if both were not *offered* them. 3. As the Holy Spirit *consecrates* and sanctifies the *waters* of baptism, giving them an *outward* and *relative* holiness; so he *consecrates* the *persons* also in an *outward* and *relative* sense, whether good or bad, by a *sacred* dedication of them to the worship and service of the *whole Trinity:* which *consecration* is for ever binding, and has its effect; either to the *salvation* of the parties, if they repent and amend, or to their greater *damnation*, if they do not. 4. I must add, that even the *unworthy* are by their baptism put into a Christian state: otherwise they would be as mere Pagans still, and would want a *new baptism* to make them Christians. Therefore, as they are by baptism translated out of their *natural* state into the state Christian, they must be supposed to have *pardon* and *grace*, and all gospel-privileges *conditionally* made over to them, though not yet *actually* applied, by reason of their disqualifications. A grant which will do them no manner of *service*,* but *hurt*, if they never repent: but if ever they do repent and turn to God, then that *conditional* grant, suspended, as it were, before, with respect to any *saving* effects, begins at length to take place effectually; and so their baptism, which had stood waiting without any *salutary* fruit for a time, now becomes *beneficial* and *saving* to the returning penitents. At the same time their *regeneration*, begun in baptism, and left unfinished, (like an *inden-*

---

* Nihil quippe profuit Simoni Mago visibilis Baptismus, cui sanctificatio invisibilis defuit. *Augustin. super Levit.* q. lxxxiv. p. 524. tom. iii.

Note, that *sanctificatio* is here used in a different meaning from what St. Austin used it in, when he spake of a *sanctification* going along with all *true* and *valid* baptism, though not *saving*. There he meant an *outward* sanctification, such as I have before described: here he means the *inward sanctification* of any one's heart and mind, necessary to make his baptism, which was before *valid*, to become *saving* also.

ture executed on one side only, or like a *part* without a *counter-part*,) comes at last to be complete, that is, actually *salutary*; not by a formal *regeneration*, (as if nothing had been done before,) but by the *repentance* of the man, and by the *sanctification* or *renovation* of the heart and mind through the *spirit*, which had been hitherto wanting.

I have now run through the *four* several *cases* proposed, observing how the affair of *regeneration* and *renovation* stands under each ; in order to give the more distinct idea of both, and to remove the main difficulties which appeared to concern either of them. From this account may be collected these particulars : 1. That *regeneration*, as containing grants of *remission, justification, adoption, covenant claim* to life eternal, is a very different notion from *renovation*, which contains only a *renewal* of *heart* and *mind*. 2. That *regeneration* is in some cases (as particularly in the case of baptized infants,) not only different in *notion*, or distinct in *theory*, but really and actually *separate* from *renovation* for the time being. 3. That in other cases, *regeneration*, while it takes in *renovation* to render it *complete* or *salutary* to the *recipient*, (and is in fact joined with it,) yet even there it differs from *renovation*, as the *whole* differs from a *part*. 4. That suppose what case, or what circumstances you please, the two *words* or *names* stand, or ought to stand, for different *notions*, for different *combinations of ideas*, and never are, or at least never ought to be, used as *reciprocal, convertible* terms. Nothing now remains, but to draw some corollaries or inferences from the general principles before laid down, by way of application, for our farther improvement.

III.

I proceed, therefore, to my *third* head of discourse, according to the method chalked out in the entrance above.

1. The first reflection I have to make, is, that it is very *improper* language at least, to call upon those who have once been *regenerated*, in their infancy, who have had their *new birth* already at the *font*, to be now regenerated ; or to bid them expect a *new birth*. Such applications might properly be directed to Jews, Turks, or Pagans, or to such *nominal* Christians as have thrown off *water-baptism:* for such really want to be *regenerated*, or *born again*, being still

in their *natural* state. But as to others, who are or have been savingly *regenerated of water* and the *spirit*, they should be called upon only to *repent* or *reform*, in order to preserve or repair that *regenerate* state which the *spirit* once gave them, and which he gave not in vain. There is no instance, no example in Scripture, (as I before hinted,) of any exhortation made to Christians, to become *regenerated*, or *born anew*, but to be *reformed* only, or *renewed* in the *inner man;* which is a very different notion from the other, as I have before manifested at large. Even Simon Magus, who had been baptized in iniquity, was not exhorted to be *regenerated* afterwards, or *born again*, but to *repent.** Our Lord himself, in the book of Revelations, made use of the like language towards the *revolting* churches; not bidding them become *regenerate*, but ordering them to *repent :*† and the wicked prophetess or sorceress, Jezebel, had time given her, not to be *regenerated* again, but to *repent.*‡ The only place I know of in Scripture that looks at all favourable to the notion of a *second* regeneration here, is a text of St. Paul's, where, writing to the *revolting* Church of Galatia, and calling them *his children*, he introduces himself under the emblem of a *pregnant* mother, and says; " My little children, of whom I travail in birth again, till Christ be formed in you."§ But then consider what an infinite difference there is between the force and import of the two *figures :* one, of a minister's *instrumentally* forming the *minds* and *manners* of his people to *faith* and *holiness;*‖ and the other, of the spirit's *authoritatively* adopting them into *divine sonship*, and into *citizenship* with all the family of heaven. The *minister's* instrumental work of *converting* or *renewing* (as even the spirit's renewing,) may often be undone, and may come over and over again : but the *regeneration of water* and the *spirit*, the *consecration* and *adoption* unto God, is quite another thing. Therefore, that *lower*

* Acts viii. 22.   † Rev. ii. 5, 16. iii. 3, 19.
‡ Rev. ii. 20, 21.   § Gal. iv. 19.
‖ See that *figure* or *emblem* explained in the *ancient* testimonies collected by Suicer, in his Thesaurus, under the word Τυτα, vol. ii. p. 1243, 1585. And compare Perkins, in answer to the objection about a *second regeneration*, as drawn from Gal. iv. 19. For though he intended his *answer* for the service of another *hypothesis*, which I have nothing to do with, yet the substance of it is true and just upon any hypothesis. See Perkins's Comment on that epistle, amongst his works, vol. ii. p. 293, 294.

sort of *sonship* of a *disciple* towards his *teacher* or *master*, may fail, and be quite extinct: but that *higher* kind of *sonship*, or *adoption*, once made in *baptism*, has an abiding force and virtue in it, and never wants to be *reiterated*, as it can never be totally *frustrated*, or made void. In short, then, the Galatians might be begotten again to St. Paul, because that meant no more than the being *reinstructed* in the faith and *reclaimed* in manners: but they could not be begotten again *to God*, unless they were to have been *rebaptized*, which the apostle had no thought of.

The mistake in this matter, I imagine, first arose from the misinterpreting some texts,* which plainly import a *water-baptism*, of an inward baptism of the *spirit* only. From hence, by degrees, *outward* baptism came to be thrown out of the idea of *regeneration*:† the next step was to confound renewal of *state* with renewal of *mind*, and so to throw the former out of the idea of *regeneration*, making it the same with what the text calls *renovation*. In a while, *conversion* and *repentance*, came to be used as terms equivalent to *regeneration:* and the consequence thence naturally following would terminate in rejecting the doctrine of *infant regeneration*, as infants are uncapable of *conversion* or *repentance:* and the next consequence to that would of course bear hard upon *infant baptism*. But that I mention by the way only, as an instance of the *gradual* alterations made in the signification of *words* or *names*, and of the *mischiefs* from thence arising. Indeed, most errors which have crept into the Church, have either been originally founded in *abuse* of *words*, or kept up by it.

* As John iii. 5. and also Tit. iii. 5.

† How mischievous this is, and how contrary to the *ancient* doctrine of *fathers*, (grounded upon *Scripture*,) may appear from the large commendations they gave of *baptism*, including *sign* and *thing:* such as *laver of life, fountain of life, garment of incorruption, key of the heavenly kingdom, water of life, living water, quickening water, heavenly donative, grace, health, life, seal, unction, choice gift of God, viaticum, pledge of resurrection, tremendous mystery,* such as *unites* us *to Christ*, makes us of the *same flesh* with him, or the *temple* of the *Holy Spirit* and of *Christ*. The authorities to this purpose are collected by Albertinus, de Eucharistia, and the places of his book are referred to in his index, under *Baptismus*. Now though those high expressions ought to be understood *cum grano salis*, in a *qualified* sense; yet certainly it is a great mistake to speak slightly of *water-baptism*, or not to take it in as the *ordinary* and *necessary*, though instrumental, cause of *regeneration, sanctification*, and perfect *renovation*.

2. Having thence shown how *improper* the language is when *Christians* are called upon to be *regenerated*, I may next observe how *mischievous* also it is in many ways, and therefore cannot be looked upon as a mere *verbal* business, or an innocent *misnomer*. 1. The telling of the common people that they ought now to be *regenerated*, which few will rightly understand, instead of telling them plainly that they ought, with the help of God's grace, speedily to *repent* and *amend*, (which is all the meaning, if it has any *good* meaning,) is giving them only a *dark* lesson instead of a *clear* one, and throwing *mists* before their eyes in a most momentous article, nearly affecting Christian practice and the spiritual life. 2. The calling upon Christians to be *regenerated*, in a new and wrong sense of the word, when they have been used to *another* and better sense in our *public* offices, and have been taught that they have been *regenerated* long ago, will not only be apt to confound their understandings, but may fill them with many a vain *scruple*, such as may give great disturbance to weak minds. 3. Another inconvenience may be, that if, instead of reminding them to preserve or repair that *regeneration* which they received in their baptism, they are called upon to receive a *second*, they may thereby be led off from looking back to their *baptismal vows*, (which are excellent lessons of true Christian piety,) and may be put upon quite another scent, nothing near so useful or edifying to them. 4. A further mischief likely to happen in that way, is, that many, instead of carefully searching into their lives past, to see wherein they have *offended*, (which is one of the first steps towards *conviction* and *remorse*, and serious *amendment*,) may be apt to go in quest of what they will call *impulses*, or *inward feelings* of the spirit; which commonly are nothing more than warm fancies, towering imaginations, and self-flattering presumptions. And this may probably take them off from a cool, careful, and impartial examination into their past life and conduct, by the safe and unerring rule of God's *written* commandments. 5. But what is worst of all, and what has frequently happened, is, that when men become more ambitious of the *honour* and *authority* which the name of the *spirit* carries with it, than of squaring their lives by the *rules* of that spirit, laid down in the gospel, they will be prone to follow any invention or imagination of their own, and will be presump-

tuous enough to father it upon the blessed spirit of God.* It is a glorious and a most desirable privilege, to be divinely inspired, divinely illuminated, divinely conducted: and as it is so honourable, and so desirable, we need not wonder if pure *self-flattery*, indulged too far, should lead many, almost *imperceptibly*, (for what more insinuating than the *illusions of* self-love?) into a serious persuasion that they themselves are the *happy favourites* of that divine spirit. How compendious a method may it seem of arriving suddenly to *deep learning* without study, and to *profound wisdom* without pain of thought; without the irksome labour of languages, history, and critical inquiries, ordinarily requisite to form a *judicious* interpreter of God's word, and a skilful guide of souls. While others are content to wait for *wisdom* till an advanced age, and in the meanwhile to go on in the *slow* methods of *labour* and *industry*, (as God has appointed,) these more early proficients affect to become wise *at once*, wise in a most *eminent* degree, at a much cheaper and easier rate. Who would not wish to be so

---

* Simon Magus, of the first age, ambitious of the *thing*, for the sake chiefly of the *name*, gave it out that he was *some great one*, Acts viii. 9. or some *great power of God*, Acts viii. 10, 18, 19. Among the Samaritans he pretended to be as the oracle of God the *Father;* among the Jews of the *Son;* and among the Gentiles of the *Holy Ghost. Iren.* lib. i. cap. 18, p. 99. Conf. Domini Massuet. pref. p. 55.

Montanus, of the second century, boasted highly and vainly of the *Spirit,* and deceived many. See Lee's History of Montanism, per tot.

Faustus the Manichee, of the fourth century, being excessively vain, was full of the like big pretences; as St. Austin observes:

Non enim *parvi* existimari se voluit, sed *Spiritum Sanctum,* consolatorem et ditatorem fidelium tuorum, auctoritate plenaria, personaliter *in se esse* persuadere conatus est. *Augustin. Confess.* lib. v. cap. 5. p. 111. ed. Bened.

Something of like kind has been perhaps in every age since. But the all-wise conduct of Divine Providence is very observable in all; that *Scripture inspiration* for seventeen hundred years has maintained its *sole* privilege; and all the other, so far as they have been considered as such, have passed off like *dreams.*

That vanity seems to have commenced first here in England, (since the reformation, I mean,) or however to have first made some figure, about a hundred years ago, set up by persons who having neither *commission*, nor *talents*, nor *furniture* proper for the *ministry*, professed themselves *saints* and *sons* of *inspiration*, as the shortest way to silence all objections, and to stop further examination. See Thomas Collier's Letters to the Saints in Taunton, (bearing date A. D. 1646.) in Edwards's Grangræna, part iii. p. 51, &c.

signally blessed, if it might be in *these days;* or if he knew
of any *certain warrant* to bear him harmless, in his making
so familiar with the *tremendous* name of the holy *spirit* of
God? But humble and modest men, who have a due *reve-*
rence for the *spirit,* and some knowledge of *themselves,* dare
not presume so far; being well aware that the setting up a
private spirit, an imaginary *inspiration,* as a rule of conduct,
has been one of the subtilest engines of Satan in all past
ages. God has permitted it, probably, for the *trial* of his
faithful servants, that they may be *proved* and *exercised* every
way; and may learn to be as much upon their guard against
any *surprise* of their understandings, as against any seduc-
tion of their *wills.* There are, as I hinted, strong tempta-
tions inclining forward men to set up their pretensions to a
private spirit. It flatters the *pride, laziness,* and *vanity* of
corrupt nature: most men love to indulge their *own* way
and humour, and to get from under the *sober standing rules*
of order, decency, and regularity. They would be their
own *masters* and *lawgivers,* and even make laws for others :
and if they can but once persuade themselves, (and what
will not blind *self-love* persuade a man into?) that they are
full of the *spirit,* they soon grow regardless of the open laws
of God and man, affecting to conduct both themselves and
others by some *secret* rules of their own breasts. This is
a very dangerous *self-deceit,* and not more *dangerous* than it
has been common in all ages and countries, as before hinted. If none but *hypocrites* or *ill-designing* men were to be
drawn into this snare, the temptation would be *coarsely* laid,
and be the less apt to deceive: but the *well-meaning* pre-
tenders to the *spirit,* who, through a secret, unperceived
self-flattery, or a complexional melancholy, first deceive
themselves, they are of all men the fittest to deceive *others..*
Their artless simplicity, their strong and endearing profes-
sions, are very apt to win upon some of the best natured
and best disposed, though unguarded Christians; which the
tempter knows full well: and he never exercises a deeper
or a more refined policy, than when he can thus decoy
some very sincere and devout Christians, in a *pious* way,
turning their *graces* into *snares,* and, as it were, foiling them
with their own artillery.

It may be useful to observe the train whereby this illu-
sion passes upon the easy credulity of less thinking per-

sons. Instead of *repentance* and *amendment* of life, (to which the world should be exhorted,) *regeneration* by the *spirit* is the phrase given out: from regeneration by the *spirit* it appears but a small and slight transition, to go on to *inspiration;* for that is a good word, when used in a just and sober sense; and it is frequently so used in our Church Liturgy.* But the word will also bear a much *higher* sense, as when ascribed to the *apostles*, or *sacred penmen;* and it is natural for self-admirers to take advantage of it, and to boast of it in an extravagant way, till at length they make their own presumptions so many dictates of the *spirit.* The final result is, the setting up a *new rule* of Christian faith, or conduct, undermining, if not directly confronting, the rule of God's *written* word laid down in the gospel.† Such has been the train, and such may be again, if we take not care to think and speak *soberly, humbly,* and *reverently* of

* In what sense *inspiration* may be justly owned, and in what not, may be clearly seen in Dr. Clagget's Treatise against Owen; Dr. Stebbing's Abridgment of it; Dr. Bennet against Quakerism; Mr. Leslie's Snake, &c. sect. xxii. p. 314, &c.

† N. B. *Scripture* and *right* reason are undoubtedly the *rule* whereby every man ought to steer; though infinite ways have been invented, either to *elude* the rule, or to *change* it into something else, under some specious *names* or colours. They that *divide* Scripture and reason more than half destroy the rule: but they that set aside *both*, for the sake of what they call *inspiration*, or *immediate revelation*, totally destroy the rule, and set up caprice and fancy, or what every body pleases, in its room.

They who contended lately for the *light of reason*, as a rule *superior* to Scripture, or as the *only* rule, and who plainly meant nothing but to bring every rule to their *own way and will;* even they were fond of the name of *inspiration* in their sense; pretending to be inspired, illuminated, or conducted by the *Spirit*, or *Holy Spirit.* See a pamphlet, entitled The Infallibility of Human Judgment; printed in 1721. p. 44, 45. See also Tindal's Christianity, &c. p. 182, 194, 330. quarto edit.

A pamphlet was published in 1731, entitled A Demonstration of the insufficiency both of Reason and Revelation: and the purport of it **was**, to intimate that *immediate inspiration* was the one thing sufficient, p. 48. Which being what every man pleases to *make* it, or to *call* by that *name*, it is obvious to see how that principle, or pretended principle, sets a man loose from true *religion* and sound *reason*, to follow his *own devices*, under those feigned *names.* All that espouse that loose principle may not perhaps *see* what it leads to, nor *mean* to push it so far: but such plainly is the *natural* tendency of it; and it has been but too often exemplified in *fact.*

what concerns the works and ways of the *divine spirit, as* we ought to do.

S. It may perhaps be expected that I should here say something upon a question heretofore raised, and often revived, about some pretended *marks* or *tokens* of *regeneration*. Those who first began to talk in that way (and who have been long dead) might be pious and well-meaning men : but they were not very happy in the *use* of their *terms*, or in the *choice* of their *marks*. They should not have asked for *marks* of *regeneration*, if they thereby meant *proofs* of a *conversion* subsequent to baptism; which it is certain they did mean : but they should have asked for *marks* of *renovation*, or of a *renewed* heart and mind. And what *marks* could a man pitch upon to satisfy *himself*, in such a case, but a *good conscience?* or what marks to satisfy *others*, but a *good life?* Then again, in drawing out their *marks*, care should have been taken to be *short* and *clear;* and more particularly to have made choice of none which many a sincere Christian may happen to want, and many a reprobate may chance to have. There was a great defect in those *marks*, that the difference of circumstances in different persons was not sufficiently considered. Some good Christians there are, (I hope many,) who have been regenerated at the font, have been so preserved and protected by God's *grace*, in conjunction with their own pious, persevering endeavours, as never to have experienced any considerable decays of the *spiritual* life, or *regenerate* state. Must they be called upon, to recollect the *day, week, month*, or *year* of their *conversion* or *regeneration*, who from their Christian infancy have never been in an *unconverted* or *unregenerate* state at all? Or must the *same* marks, (suppose of strong conviction, fearful compunction, stinging remorse, nigh to despair, and the like) be sought for in such persons, who have loved and served God sincerely all their days; and who have found religion and righteousness to sit so easy upon them, (as God's service is perfect freedom) that they have been all along strangers to those pangs, struggles, conflicts, which ungodly men must of course feel in the correcting their evil habits, upon their conversion to godliness? Those pretended marks are manifestly too *particular* to serve all cases, and too *uncertain* to be depended on in any : they appear to have a tendency to *perplex* some, and to *deceive* others; and therefore may prudently be thrown aside as things of *human invention;** and in the mean while it will be safe and right to have recourse to *divine law.* Ask our Lord for a *mark* of a true disciple, and his resolution lies in few words, short and full: " If ye love me, keep my commandments:† that is his *mark* of what some call *regeneration.* If you consult St. Paul upon the same point, he will say, " As many as are led by the Spirit of God, they are the sons of God:"‡ and, "The fruit of the spirit is love, joy, peace, long-suffering, gentleness, goodness, faith, meekness, temperance: against such there is no law."§ If you ask St. John, who seems to have written a good part of his First Epistle on purpose to confute some of his own time, who vainly boasted of being *born of God,* while they took no care to maintain *good works;*‖ I say, if you consult him, he will tell you, " Whosoever is born of God doth not commit sin:" and, "In this the children of God are manifest, and the children of the devil: whosoever doth not righteousness is not of God."¶ The man is known by his *heart* and *life,* tried by the rule of God's *commandments.* These are unerring, infallible, *marks;* marks which every *good* Christian has, and every *bad* one wants. But if any scruple should remain about the *application* of this rule to every one's conscience, (because we have all of us *infirmities,* and " in many things we offend all,")** the *safest* rule whereby to judge of our own particular state, as to conform to the *Scripture rule,* I conceive to be this: if we sincerely

* See more of what concerns the pretended *marks* of *regeneration* in an excellent sermon of Archbishop Sharpe, vol. iii. serm. xiii. p. 299, &c.

† John xiv. 15.   ‡ Rom. viii. 14.   § Gal. v. 22, 23.

‖ They seem to have been the Simonians, who, among other monstrous opinions, taught that men are saved by *grace* only, and not according to their *good works. Secundum enim ipsius gratiam salvari homines, sed non secundum operas justas. Iren.* lib. i. c. 23. p. 100. ed. Bened. Conf. Theodorit. Hæret. Fab. lib. i. c. 1. Bull's Harmon. dissert. i. p. 419. alias p. 13. diss. ii. p. 438. alias 33.

¶ John iii. 9, 10. "'Ο ποιων την αμαρτιαν, *one that makes sin, a sin maker:* and on the other side, he, the general course and tenor of whose life and conversation is upright and unblameable, is called ο ποιων την δικαιοσυνην, *one that makes righteousness.*——By the first, we understand one who *gives his mind to sin, and makes a practice of it.* By the latter, we understand one who *gives himself wholly to virtue,* and makes it his *aim* and *study* to live a *good life.*" *Bishop Blackall, on the sermon on the mount,* vol. i. serm. x. p. 335.   ** James iii. 2.

take care to do the *best* we *can*, are daily gaining ground of our *vices* and our *passions*, and find ourselves, after the strictest examination, to be upon the *improving* hand, then may we comfortably believe that our *regeneration* yet abides, *salutary* and *entire*, and that we are in a state of *grace* and *salvation.**

But, above all things, beware of ever trusting to *inward feelings, secret impulses*, or the like, as *marks* of a good state, till you have thoroughly tried and examined them by the unerring rule of God's *written* word. What are any *impulses*, considered barely in themselves, but some *strong inclinations, motions*, or *affections*, which men feel in their breasts, and cannot presently distinguish from the *natural* workings of their own minds? But suppose them by their unusual *strength*, or *warmth*, or their *uncommon manner* of affecting us, to import something *supernatural* or *extraordinary*, (I only make the supposition, not affirming that *supernatural* motions are often, or in these days, so distinguished,) then consider, that there are *evil spirits* to tempt and deceive, as well as a *good spirit* to enlighten and sanctify; and there is no certain way of knowing (without well considering the nature and tendency, the justice or injustice of what we are *moved* to,) from whence the *impulse* cometh. Judas probably had a *strong impulse* upon him to betray his Lord; for Satan had *entered* into him.†‍ What *fair colours* the tempter might lay before him, to calm a rebuking conscience, and whether he might not persuade him, that it would be only giving our Lord an opportunity of setting forth his divine power and glory in his own *rescue*.‡ is more than we can certainly know: but *self-flattery* is apt enough to invent or to lay hold on *soft colourings* and *good meanings;* and there is scarce any wickedness whatever, but what is capable of being so *varnished* by a subtile wit. Ananias was perhaps another instance of *strong impulses*, moving him to "lie to the Holy Ghost," (a grievous sin and near akin to " lying of the Holy Ghost.")§

* Compare Archbishop Sharpe's larger resolution of the same case, vol. iii. serm. xiii. p. 300, 301, 305, 306.

† Luke xxii. 3. John xiii. 2, 27.

‡ See Dr. Whitby's Comment on Matth. xxvii. 3.

§ The confident reporting a fact which nearly concerns the *Holy Ghost*, by a person who *knows not* that *fact* to be a *truth*, is so like the calling upon God as *witness* to a *false*, or at least a *doubtful* fact, that

Satan had " filled his heart."*   He also might have been
deceived by *good meanings*, such as the tempter had art-
fully suggested, and thrown as *mists* before his eyes: but
the thing was *evil in itself*, and he ought to have known it.
It is certain that the *persecutors* of the church of Christ,
some of them at least, had a very *good meaning* in it, "thinking to do God service"† by it: yet nobody can doubt but
that they therein acted *wickedly:* and we have warrant sufficient from the general rule of Scripture (that " he that
committeth sin is of the devil")‡ to say that they were
moved and *actuated* by *Satan* in what they so did, though
with a *zeal* for *God* and a *pious* intention to serve him.
Therefore again, it is exceeding dangerous to trust either
to *warm impulses* or to *godly intentions*, without first strictly inquiring into the *nature* of the acts, and into the *law-
fulness* of the *means* to be made use of for compassing the
end aimed at. If any man " does evil that good may come,"
he is a *transgressor:* it is acting *wickedly* for God, and dis-
honouring him most highly, in attempting to serve him by *sin*.
Pious intentions or godly aims will never bear a man out in
unwarrantable practices: the *end* must be *good*, and the *means*
also, or else the action is *wicked*, and the man an *ungodly*
man.   Therefore, at last, as I before hinted, there is no
safe rule to go by, but the rule of *right* reason in conjunction with God's *written* word : by these every *impulse* must
be scanned and tried, both as to *end* and *means*, before we
can pass any certain judgment of it, whether it comes from
Satan, (if it be really *supernatural*)§ or from the *spirit* of
God.   If God *in the soul* (as some term it) commands any
thing contrary to *God in the Bible*, as, for instance, to be
disobedient to lawful superiors in things good or lawful, to
break comely *order* and *regularity*, (on which depends the
very *life* of religion and the *being* of a church,) or to *invade*

I scarce see how to distinguish it, or how to excuse it from being
equally criminal. There cannot however be too much *caution* used in
matters of that *high* nature, so nearly affecting the honour of the *tremendous* Deity.   * Acts v. 3, 4.
    † John xvi. 2. Acts xxvi. 9.   ‡ 1 John iii. 8. John viii. 44.
    § I put in that restriction, as being aware of a middle opinion, which
looks upon most of those cases as *compassionate* cases, arising from
some unhappy *distemper* of mind, some *complexional* disorder.   See
Meric Casaubon concerning enthusiasm, printed A. D. 1655. and Dr.
Henry More's Enthusiasmus triumphatus, printed in 1656.

other men's provinces, or so much as to *take offence* if not permitted to do so: or, if the supposed *God in the soul* is observed to blow men up with *spiritual* pride and *self-admiration*, and a supercilious *contempt* of others, teaching them to reject all remonstrances of sound *reason* to the contrary, as *carnal reason*,* and all remonstrances offered from *Scripture* as coming merely from *natural* men, (which is, in short, resolving to stop their ears against *Scripture* and *reason*, to follow their own fancies;) I say, if the supposed *God in the soul* either prescribes such practices, or instils such principles of error and confusion; then may we be assured, that it is not the *God of heaven* that does it, but the "God of this world," (if any) which sometimes "blinds the minds of them that believe not, lest the glorious gospel of Christ," (the *sovereign* rule of Christian faith and conduct) "should shine upon them."† Great care should be taken, not to invert the right order of things, not to begin at the wrong end. Say not, *we are favourites of heaven, we have the spirit, therefore our hearts are right, and our ways good;* for that would be drawing a very *precarious* conclusion from *dark* and *disputable* premises: but say rather, (after *impartial* examination,) *our hearts are right, and our ways good, and therefore we have the spirit.* For he that is *led* by the spirit, and *walks* by the *written* rules of the spirit, he, and he only, can, upon sure grounds, say, that he *has the spirit.*‡ And when he can say it, let him

---

* See the pamphlet before mentioned, entitled, A Demonstration of the Insufficiency both of Reason and Revelation, p. 48—54. And compare Dr. Bennet's Confutation of Quakerism, (chap. v. p. 44—61.) in answer to the fond pretences raised from a *mistaken* distinction between the *natural* and *spiritual* man: a distinction, as by some used, contrived only to fence against all conviction or persuasion; and to set up that monstrous *infallibility* in every *private* man's breast, which is justly detested by all sober men, when pretended to by any *public* person, or by any *collective* body of men whatsoever. † 2 Cor. iv. 4.

‡ Rom. viii. 1. i. 4, 5, 14. Gal. v. 16, 18. To the *law and to the testimony: if they speak not according to this word, it is because there is no light in them.* Isaiah viii. 20.

Hence it appears that God's ordinary way of enlightening men is by the *outward* word written, and not by his *immediate* teaching or inspiration, without such *outward* means. The *spirit's* work is the *opening* and *disposing* the hearts of men to receive instruction from the *written* word; to improve by *mediate* (not *immediate*,) revelation. See Whitby's Comment on James i. 18. p. 678, 679.

say it to *himself*, and to God, (whom he ought to thank for
so inestimable a blessing,) and let him not rashly *boast* of
it* before the world, nor censoriously *judge* or *despise* others;
for that would be directly copying after the *proud Pharisee*,
and would infallibly *quench* the spirit. Common *modesty*
and *decency*, and above all, our *common Christianity*, forbids
all such *boasting* of the ordinary *graces;* which would amount
to the same with blazing it abroad, how *pure*, how *holy*, how
righteous we take ourselves to be, above others. Neither
will it avail us, in such cases, to urge that we *know* it, and
that we *thank God* for it, ascribing nothing to *ourselves:*
for did not even the proud Pharisee do the same, when he
said, "God, I thank thee that I am not as other men are!"†
&c. Christianity is an humble, quiet, peaceable, and order-
ly religion; not noisy or ostentatious, not assuming or cen-
sorious, not factious or tumultuous: they who think otherwise of it, are altogether strangers to it, and know nothing
yet, as they ought to know, of the life and spirit of true
Christianity.

4. And here, in the next place, it may not be amiss to
throw in some few thoughts concerning a *passionate* religion, and the nature or danger of it. Indeed all our *passions* ought to centre in God, and they can never be better
spent than upon his glory and service. But *passion*, even
in that case, without *reason, judgment*, or sound *discretion*,
in the use of *just* and *proper* means, works in like manner
as any other wild and turbulent passion does; for *passion*,
as such, is *blind*. *Violent* passions and unruly affections
are the worst guides imaginable, whether in *religion* or in
any other affairs of *moment*. For like as an over zealous
and over officious *admirer* often forgets the good counsel
of a *wise* friend whom he undertakes to serve, overlooks

---

* I said *rashly*, to exclude some very *rare* and *extraordinary* cases,
where a person may *commend* himself. St. Paul did so: but then he
knew that what he said was strictly *true:* he *knew* that there was a very
great *necessity* for it: he *knew* that he had *God's warrant* for so doing
in that case, writing by *inspiration*, and able to give *miraculous proof*
of *Christ speaking in him:* he did it not for *pre-eminence* over *true* apostles, but to hinder *false* apostles from assuming a pre-eminence *over*
him, to the *destruction* of *Christianity:* those were circumstances,
which so justify his *self-commendation*, as to leave every other, if in
different circumstances, or *differently* managed, without excuse.

† Luke xviii. 11.

his instructions, disturbs all his affairs, crosses his interests, exposes his reputation, and makes it at length necessary for his friend to discard him for his ill-managed fondness: so a heady, unthinking *religionist*, through his *eagerness* and *impatience* in the cause of God, often forgets God's *sacred laws*, and overlooks his all-wise *commandments;* and in conclusion, rather disturbs, obstructs, and exposes religion than serves it; and therefore cannot reasonably expect a *reward* for it. True religion requires both a *warm* heart and a *cool* head; especially in a *minister* of it, if he proposes to do any good service in his function. It is easy for warm zealots to throw reflections upon the wiser and more considerate guides, who come not up to their degrees of *intemperate* heat and ferment: but a small knowledge of mankind will suffice to show, that they who will not be converted by cool, calm, and rational measures, will not be wrought upon as to any good and lasting effect, by eagerness or passion. The world, indeed, is generally *bad*, always was, and always will be: but still we must not venture upon affected, irregular, unjustifiable courses, in order to reclaim it; which in reality would not *reclaim* it, but make it *worse*. Men must be brought to God, in God's own way, if at all. When the ministers of Christ have done all that was *just, prudent,* or *proper*, and the effect does not answer, they must not presume to grow as *mad* in one way, as *sinners* are in another, in hopes to recover them to their *senses*. Is any man zealous for the Lord God of hosts? It is well that he is so. But still there is one thing of as great, or greater importance than any, and which ought to be looked to in the *first* place; namely, to rest contented with God's *approved* and *authorized* methods of *reforming* the world; to submit to his *wisdom* rather than our *own;* to proceed no farther than God has *warranted;* but to *stop* where God requires it, as well as to *run* where he has *sent*. God will be served, as becomes an *awful* Governor of the universe, not with *amorous* freedoms or *fond* familiarities, but with reverence and respectful fear; at a becoming *distance*, in due form and solemnity, and with the strictest *order* and *regularity*. He struck Uzzah with death for his over officiousness;[*] condemned Saul for intermeddling where he had nothing to do;[†] and reproved the prophets, or pretended prophets, for pro-

---

[*] 2 Sam. vi. 7. 1 Chron. xiii. 9, 10.   [†] 1 Sam. xiii. 9—14.

A SUMMARY VIEW

OF THE

DOCTRINE OF JUSTIFICATION.

THE doctrinal points of *regeneration* and *renovation* have been lately brought upon the carpet; and I have, upon another occasion, taken the liberty to throw in some few thoughts upon them. Now the subject *of justification* being nearly allied to the former, and seeming also to want some farther illustrating, by way of appendage or supplement to the points before mentioned; my present design is to give you a *summary view* of it, by considering,

I. What the *name* imports.

II. What the *thing* contains.

III. How it stands *distinguished* from renovation and regeneration.

IV. What are the *concurring causes* on God's part, and on man's, to produce it, and to preserve it.

V. What are the common *extremes* which many have been apt to run into on this head, and how they may be avoided.

I.

The first article is the *name*, which ought to be defined before the *thing;* and, in order thereto, must be first distinguished.

There appears to be sufficient ground in *Scripture* for distinguishing *justification* into *active* and *passive:* for as the name *regeneration*, when denoting an *act* or *grant* of God, bears an *active* sense, and when denoting a *privilege* received by *us*, bears a *passive* sense; such also is the case with respect to the name *justification*. It means either God's grant, for it is *God* that *justifies;*[*] or it means *our privilege*,

---

[*] Rom. iii. 25, 26, 30. iv. 5. viii. 33. Gal. iii. 8. Tit. iii. 7. Rom. iv. 25. v. 18. N. B. In the two last texts, the word for *justification* is *δικαιωσις*, which bears an *active* sense.

endowment, possession holden of God,* as we are said to be *justified* by him. *Justification* always supposes *two parties*, one to *give*, and another to *receive;* whether *without any act* at all on the *receptive* side, as in the case of *infants*, or whether *accompanied* with *receptive acts*, as in the case of *adults*, who may be properly said to *accept* and *assent* to, as well as to receive or enjoy. God, the supreme lawgiver, may be considered either as a *rector* and *governor*, *contracting* with *man*, and laying down the *terms* of his *covenant;* or as a *judge*, giving *sentence* according to the *terms laid down.* Correspondently, *man* may be considered either as *accepting* the terms upon his *entering into covenant;* or as *pleading* them afterwards at the *bar of justice*, at the divine tribunal. There is no more difference between those two several views of the same thing, than there is between the *issuing out a general grant* for the *benefit* of all persons who shall duly and properly *accept* it, and the *actual conferring* the *benefit of that grant* upon the persons *so accepting:* but some have chosen *one* view for the easier and apter explaining (as they conceived,) the nature of *justification;* and some have preferred the *other,* for the like reasons.† The general way has been to understand *justification* as a kind of *law term,* expressing a *judicial* transaction. *Protestants* of every denomination have set themselves to defend it :‡ and even *Romanists* also, many of them, have readily submitted to it.§ So that the

---

* Δικαιοσυνη, which may as well be rendered *justification* as *righteousness*, appears to mean *our righteousness*, which we hold of *God's grace* by faith in Christ Jesus, in the following texts; Rom. i. 17. iii. 5, 21, 22. ix. 30, 31. x. 3. 1 Cor. i. 30. 2 Cor. v. 21. Philip. iii. 9. 2 Pet. i. 1. Matt. vi. 33.

† "It is indeed to be granted, that *justification* importeth, not making of a man righteous, but declaring him and accounting him righteous, treating him and dealing with him as righteous: all this is true; and yet I will not grant that it is so properly understood to be the act of God as sitting upon the throne of *judgment,* (whether according to mercy or justice,) as the act of God *contracting* with man for everlasting life, upon condition of submitting to the covenant of grace, and the terms of it." *Thorndike Epil.* book ii. p. 40. Conf. Puffendorf. Jus. Fecial. Divin. p. 144, 166, 172, 319, 349, 353.

‡ Bishop Andrew's Serm. p. 76. Field, p. 291. Bishop Bull, p. 411, &c. Prid. Spanhem. Fil. tom. iii. p. 276. Vitringa, Observat. Sacr. lib. iv. c. 10. sect. 6. &c. tom. i. p. 346. Buddæus, Instit. Theol. p. 951. Deylingius, Obs. Sacr. tom. iii. p. 561.

§ Vid. Gul. Forbes, Consid. Modest. p. 98. edit. 2.

word *justification*, in this view, and in the *active* sense, will signify *God's pronouncing* a person *just*, and his *accepting* him *as such*,* while, in the *passive* sense, it will signify *man's* being *so declared*, and thereupon *accepted* into new privileges, and his enjoying the benefits thereof.† So much for the *name*.

II.

I am *next* to consider what the *thing* granted and received *really is*, or what it *contains*.

Here we are to observe, not barely what the *word* itself strictly and grammatically *signifies*, but what it *stands for*, and must stand for, as made use of in this *particular* case, or in such and such *circumstances*. The *evangelical notion* of it must be governed by *evangelical principles*: it is a *complex notion*, which takes in *more ideas* than the *name* would *necessarily* signify in *different circumstances*.

1. *Remission of sins* is most certainly one *considerable part*, or ingredient, of *evangelical justification*: not that the *name*, abstractedly considered, imports it, but the *nature of the thing*, in this case, *requires* it. Had our *first parents* preserved their *innocence* entire, they would have been thereupon *justified* as *inherently* and *perfectly just*, needing no *pardon*: but men in a *lapsed state*, being all of them more or less *sinners*, cannot be accepted as persons who *have had no sin*, but as persons *discharged* from it. I need not here say, *how*, or upon *what account*; because that will be considered hereafter in its proper place: but in the mean time it is self-evident, that the *justification* of a *sinner* must include *remission of sin*. I may add, that such *remission of sin* properly signifies a *discharge from the penalty* due to it; not from the *blame* it carries with it; except it be in such a sense as Zacharias and Elizabeth were pronounced *blameless*;‡ for so all *good Christians*, living up to the *gospel terms*, and persevering to the end, will be pronounced *blame-*

---

* Justificatio evangelica quæ *Deum auctorem* respicit, definiri potest, *actio Dei* qua pœnitentem absolvit, propter *merita* Christi *viva* fide accepta et applicata. *Fogg. Theolog. Speculat. Schema*, p. 427.

† Si consideretur (justificatio) cum respectu ad conditionem *justificati*, est *mutatio status*, quem resipiscens obtinet erga Deum, unde cessante reatu, propter merita Christi *viva* fide applicata, non est condemnationi obnoxius. *Ibid.* p. 427, 428.   ‡ Luke i. 6.

less at the last day: and so are they esteemed of here, in the mean season, by God, who searches the hearts.*

2. But, besides *remission of sin*, a *right* and *title* to life eternal, but founded only upon *promise*,† is included in the *gospel notion* of *justification:* not that the bare force of the *word* requires it, (for a man might be properly said to be *justified*, who is *acquitted* from *penalty*, though not entitled to a *reward*,) but we know what the *Scripture promises* are; and that a *discharge from penalty* hath thereby a sure *title to rewards* connected with it: therefore *evangelical justification* comprehends, according to the *full notion* of it, not only a *title to pardon*, but a *title to salvation* also, a title to both for the time being.‡

3. To these some learned divines have added the *sanctification* of the *Holy Spirit*,§ as a *third ingredient*, to complete the nature or notion of *justification:* but that persuasion is scarce tenable, unless we first qualify it with proper *distinctions.* If by *sanctification* we understand *renovation* of the *inward* man, *that* has no place in the *justification* of *infants;* besides that even in *adults* it is rather a *qualification for* the privilege, than the *privilege itself:* but if by *sanctification* of the spirit be meant only the baptismal *unction*, or that *sealing* of the *spirit*,‖ which goes along with all *valid*, and of course with all *saving* baptism;¶ *that* indeed must necessarily be supposed in all baptismal *justification*, as a part of it, or an ingredient in it; inasmuch as *justification* cannot be conceived without some work of the *spirit* in conferring a *title to salvation.* In this sense, every person *justified* is *ipso facto* sealed and consecrated by the *spirit* of God. But the truth of this matter will more fully appear under another head in the sequel.

* Vid. Grab. in Annotatis ad Bulli Opp. p. 414. edit. ult.

† *Debitor* enim factus est [Deus] non aliquid a nobis *accipiendo*, sed quod ei placuit promittendo. Aliter enim dicimus homini *debes mihi quia dedi tibi;* et aliter dicimus, *debes mihi quia promisisti mihi.*——Illo ergo modo possumus exigere dominum nostrum, ut dicamus, redde quod *promisisti*, quia fecimus quod *jussisti:* et hoc *tu fecisti*, quia laborantes juvisti. *Augustin.* serm. clviii. de verbis Apost. Rom. viii. p. 762. tom. v. edit. Bened.

‡ Vid. Bull. Exam. Censur. ad Animadv. iii. p. 537, 538.

§ Vid. Gul. Forbes, Consid. Modest. p. 118, &c.

‖ See Bingham xi. 1, 6.　　　　　¶ See Regeneration Stated.

III.

Having thus briefly considered *what justification is,* and *what it contains;* I proceed to observe how it is *distinguished* from *renovation* and *regeneration,* to both which it is indeed very nearly allied.

1. By *renovation* I understand the *inward renewing* of the *heart and mind;** the same that commonly goes under the name of inward *sanctification* of the *spirit.* This is necessarily presupposed, in some measure or degree, with respect to *adults,* in their *justification;* because without holiness no man shall see the Lord,"† no man shall be *entitled to salvation;* that is to say, no man *justified.* But though this consideration sufficiently proves that *sanctification* and *justification* are *near allied;* yet it does not prove that they are the *same thing,* or that one is properly *part* of the other. An *essential qualification* for any *office, post, dignity,* or *privilege,* must be supposed to *go along* with that *office, post,* &c.; but still the *notions* are very *distinct,* while the *things* themselves are in fact *connected* of course. So stands the case between *sanctification* and *justification:* the one is a *capacity for* such a grant; the other is the *very grant* itself: the one is an *infused* and *inherent quality,* God's work *within* us; the other, an *outward privilege,* or *extrinsic relation,* God's gracious act *towards* us. In short, *sanctification* denotes the *frame of mind,* the holy disposition; while *justification* denotes the *state* which a man is in with respect to God, his *discharge from guilt and penalty,* his *Christian membership,* his *heavenly citizenship,* his *gospel rights, pleas,* and *privileges.*

Again: *sanctification* is commonly understood of the *mind,* or *soul,* only; while *justification* is of the *whole man.* The title which the *body* hath to a future *resurrection* or *redemption,* is included in the very notion of a *justified* man.

It may be further noted, that *justification may be supposed,* where *sanctification* (according to the full notion thereof,) *is not;* as in the case of *infants* newly baptized : they are indeed thereby *sanctified* in a certain sense; but not in the sense of a proper *renewal* of *mind and heart.* These considerations sufficiently mark out the *difference* between *justification* and *sanctification.*

2. I am *next* to observe, how *justification* differs from *re-*

---

* See Regeneration Stated.   † Hebr. xii. 14.

generation. They *differ* but little as to the *main things;* since the *grants* made, and the *blessings* conferred, are much the *same in both:* but still there is *some* difference, and that both *notional* and *real.*

So far as the *main things* are the *same,* they are however expressed under *different figures:* for in *regeneration,* God is considered as a *Father* begetting us into a new life of light, blessings, and privileges: but in *justification,* he is considered either as a *proprietor* making over the same grants, or as a *judge* giving favourable sentence from the throne of mercy.

Another *difference* is, that *regeneration,* in the strict sense, expresses no more than the *first admittance* and *entrance* into such and such rights and privileges; and therefore comes but *once:* but *justification* is a thing *continued** during the whole spiritual life: one is giving and receiving *life;* the other is giving and receiving *growth* and *increase.*

A third *difference* is, that *regeneration,* in the stricter sense† of that name, may admit of the distinction of *salutary,* and *not salutary:* whereas *justification* admits not of that distinction at all, being *salutary* in the *very notion* of it, as it imports a *right* and *title to salvation,* for the time being, on the *gospel terms.*

A fourth *difference* is, that *regeneration,* once given and received, can never be *totally lost,* any more than baptism, nor ever want to be reiterated in the *whole* thing:‡ but *justification* may be *granted* and *accepted,* and *take place* for a time, and yet may *cease* afterwards, both *totally* and *finally.§* These

---

* Vid. Gul. Forbes, p. 261. Bulli Op. p. 437. and compare my Review of the Doctrine of the Eucharist, vol. vii. p. 238, 242, 253, 265.

† Of the *stricter* and *larger* sense of the word *regeneration,* see Regeneration Stated.

St. Austin followed the *stricter* sense when he said, Simon ille Magus natus erat ex aqua et Spiritu, tom. ix. p. 169.

In another place, he followed the *larger* sense, which takes in *renovation* to complete the notion of regeneration considered as *salutary.*

Qui *natus est ex Deo* habet caritatem—videat si habeat caritatem, et tunc dicat, *natus sum ex Deo.*——Habeat caritatem; aliter non se dicat *natum* ex Deo. *Augustin.* tom. iii. part. ii. p. 859.

Hence it appears, that as the word *faith* sometimes signifies simply *faith,* and sometimes *saving faith,* so the word *regeneration* admits of the like twofold meaning.

‡ See Regeneration Stated.

§ See Article XVI. and Homily on Good Works. Compare Bulli Op. p. 668. Augustin. Conf. c. xi. Truman, Great Propit. p. 153,

several articles of *difference* sufficiently show that the *names* are not tantamount, but that they stand for *things different;* *similar* in *some* respects only, not in *all.*

IV.

Having considered *what justification is,* and *how distinguished,* I may now pass on to inquire into its *constituent causes, principal* and *less principal, efficient* and *instrumental, divine* and *human,* and the like: for there are *several causes,* more or less contributing to the *justification* of a person; that is, to the making him a *sure title to salvation* for the time being.

1. *God the Father* is here to be considered as *principal,* as he is the head and fountain of all. Of that there can be no question, and therefore I need not say more of it: the *Divine philanthropy* is of *prime consideration* in the whole thing.

2. In the next place, *God the Son* is here to be considered as the *procuring* and *meritorious cause* of *man's justification,* both by his *active* and *passive* obedience.* This, though it may be disputed by such as will dispute any thing, or every thing, yet seems to be generally admitted among the sober divines of all the great divisions of *Christians.*

3. In the third place, *God the Holy Ghost* is here to be considered as the *immediate, efficient cause:* for proof of which, we need go no farther than our Lord's own words, that, "except one be born of water and of the spirit, he cannot enter into the kingdom of God;† which is as much, as to say, he cannot have a *title* to salvation, cannot be *jus-*

178. Heylin. Histor. Quinquartic. part i. p. 17, 28, 33, 86. part iii. p. 31, &c.

The sense of our church on this head is manifest from this single consideration; that she looks upon it as *certain by God's word,* that all *children baptized* are so far *justified,* inasmuch as if they *die* before *actual sin,* they are *undoubtedly saved.* Now it cannot be doubted but that many who have been baptized in *infancy,* may, and do fall afterwards, both *totally* and *finally:* therefore our church must of consequence allow and suppose, that persons once *justified* may *totally* and *finally* perish.

* See Gul. Forbes, Consider. Modest. p. 67, &c. Thorndike Epil. book ii. p. 254, &c. Puffendorf. Jus. Fecial. p. 187.

† John iii. 5. Comp. 1 Cor. vi. 11. xii. 13. Tit. iii. 5, 6, 7.

tified. Neither need we here put in the restriction *or-dinarily* so far as the *spirit* is concerned: his *immediate agency* must be supposed, in *all cases,* and upon *every sup-position.*

4. After the three *divine persons,* principally concurring and co-operating in *man's justification,* we may next pass on to the *subordinate instruments:* and here come in the *ministry,* the *word,* and the *sacraments;** but more particu-larly the sacrament of *baptism;* which perhaps may here deserve a *large* and *distinct consideration,* as it has been too often *omitted,* or but *perfunctorily* mentioned, in treatises written upon the subject of *justification.*

If we look either into the *New Testament,* or into the *an-cient fathers,* we shall there find that the *sacrament of bap-tism,* considered as a *federal rite* or *transaction* between God and man, is either declared or supposed the ordinary, ne-cessary, outward *instrument* in God's hands of man's *jus-tification:* I say an instrument in *God's* hands, because it is certain, that in that sacred rite, *God himself bears a part,*† as *man also bears his;* and that *in* both *sacraments* (as our church teaches,) "God embraces us, and offereth himself to be embraced by us."‡ According to the natural order of *precedency,* the authorized *ministry* is *first* in consideration;§ the *word* next; then *hearing,* and *believing* with a penitent heart and lively faith; after that, *baptism,* and therein the first solemn and certain *reception* of *justification,* which is afterwards *continued* by the same *lively faith,* and the use of the *word,* and of the other *sacrament.*

Now, as to *baptism,* and its being, ordinarily, the neces-sary *outward mean* or *instrument* of *justification,* the *imme-diate* and *proximate form* and *rite of conveyance;* that will be easily made appear from many clear texts of the *New Tes-*

---

* Sacramenta sunt *media* offerentia et exhibentia *ex parte Dei:* fides *medium* recipiens et apprehendens ex *parte nostra. Gerhard. Loc. Comm.* part. iv. p. 309.

Tantum dicimus, quemadmodum *fides* est quasi *manus nostra,* qua nos quærimus et accipimus; sic *verbum* et *sacramenta* esse quasi *manus Dei,* quibus is nobis offert et confert quod fide a nobis petitur et acci-pitur. *Vossius de Sacram. VI et Effic.* Op. tom. vi. p. 252.

† See Review of the Doctrine of the Eucharist, vol. vii. p. 14, &c.
‡ Homily on the Common Prayer and Sacraments.
§ Rom. x. 13, 14, 15. Tit. i. 3.

tament, as also from the concurring verdict of *antiquity*, the best interpreter of the sacred writings.

First. The *texts* I shall here take in their *order*. " He that believeth and is baptized shall be saved; but he that believeth not shall be damned."* Here the word *saved* amounts to the same thing in the main with *justified*, being opposed to condemned : and it is farther observable, that the believing here must be understood of a lively faith; yet that alone, is not said to save, or justify, but with the addition of *baptism*, or in and with the use of *baptism* : for whatever some may please to teach of *faith only* as *justifying*, the *exclusive term*, most certainly, is not to be understood in opposition, either to the *work* of the *Father*, or of the *Son* or of the *Holy Ghost;* or to the standing *means* of conveyance which they have chosen. The warmest contenders for faith alone, are content to admit that the exclusive term, *alone*, is opposed only to every thing else on *man's part* in *justifying*, not to any thing on *God's part* : now I have already noted that *baptism* is an *instrument* in *God's* hand, who *bears his part* in it; and, therefore, *baptism*, in this view, relates to God's part in *justifying*, and not to *man's*. It is not indeed said in the text just cited, that he who is not *baptized* shall be *damned*, as it is said of him who *believeth not*. God reserves to himself a liberty of dispensing in that case. At the same time, he has made no promise or covenant to *justify* any one *without* the use of *baptism :* so that still *baptism* must be looked upon as the *ordinary* standing *instrument* of *justification* on *God's part;* and we have no certain warrant for declaring any one *justified* independently of it.

The next remarkable *text* is, " Except one be born of water and of the spirit, he cannot enter into the kingdom of God, cannot see the kingdom of God."† Where we may observe, that born again, in the second verse, is interpreted of *baptism*, (*sign* and *thing signified*,) in the fifth; and the emphatical word, *cannot*, is twice made use of in that case. What room then is there left for pretending any direct and positive promise from God to *justify* any man *before*, or *without* that *ordinary mean ?* Say that faith is our instrument for receiving justification, which is saying enough; still *baptism* must be *God's instrument*, ordinarily, for applying or con-

* Mark xvi. 16.   † John iii. 3, 5. See Regeneration Stated.

E

ferring it, in virtue of what our Lord himself, in that place, has *twice* solemnly declared. But I pass on.

In the second of the Acts, we read these words of St. Peter to the Jews of that time; " Repent and be baptized every one of you in the name of Jesus Christ for the remission of sins, and ye shall receive the gift of the Holy Ghost."* Now it is to be noted, that true repentance, in such case, *pre-supposes* some degrees of preparatory *grace* and *lively faith;* and yet *baptism* was to *intervene* too, in order to *remission*, that is, in order to *justification*, and the gift of the indwelling of the Holy Spirit of God.

So again in the case of St. Paul, at his conversion to Christianity: he had been a *true believer* from the time when he said, " Lord, what wilt thou have me to do ?"†   But he **was** not yet *justified:* his sins remained in charge for *three days* at least longer: for it was so long before Ananias came to him, and said, "Arise and be baptized, and wash away thy sins, calling on the name of the Lord."‡   *Baptism* was at length his grand absolution, his patent of *pardon*, his instrument of *justification* granted him from above: neither was he *justified* till he *received that Divine seal*, inasmuch as his sins were upon him *till that very time*.

Pass we on to the epistle to the Romans, where St. Paul says; " Know ye not, that so many of us as were baptized into Jesus Christ, were baptized into his death ?" (that is, into a participation of the *death* and *merits* of Christ, through which also we *die* unto sin.)   " Therefore we are buried with him by baptism into death."§   In *baptism* is the first formal solemn death unto sin, in the *plenary remission* of it; which comes to the same as to say, that there also *commences* our *justification* entire : all before was but preparatory to it, as conception is to the *birth*.||

The same St. Paul says; "By one spirit are we all baptized into one body."¶   Now if we are first *incorporated* into the *mystical* body of Christ by *baptism*, it is manifest that we are there also first *justified:* for no man strictly belongs to Christ till he is incorporated ; neither is any one

---

* Acts ii. 38.   † Acts ix. 6.   ‡ Acts xxii. 16.
§ Rom. vi. 3, 4. See Wolfius in loc.

‖ Fiunt ergo *inchoationes* quædam fidei, *conceptionibus* similes: non tamen solum *concipi*, sed etiam *nasci* opus est, ut ad vitam perveniatur æternam. *Augustin. de Divers. Quæst. ad Simplic.* tom. vi. lib. i. p. 89.

¶ 1 Cor. xii. 13. See my Review, &c., vol. vi. p. 269, &c.

justified before he is incorporated, and made a member of Christ, a citizen of heaven.

St. Paul also says; " Ye are all the children of God by faith in Christ Jesus. For as many of you as have been baptized into Christ have put on Christ."* Words very observable, as plainly intimating, that ordinarily a person is not made a child of God by *faith*, till that faith is *exerted* in, and perfected by *baptism*. *Faith* in adults is the hand whereby they receive the privilege of *adoption* and *justification;* while the sacrament is the hand whereby God dispenses it.

God is the donor, and he can dispense the grace to some without *faith*, as to *infants;* and to others without *baptism*, as to martyrs principally, and to catechumens prevented by extremities: but still the *ordinary* rule is, first to dispense it upon a *true* and *lively faith*, sealed with the *stipulations* mutually passed in *baptism*.

So again, we read in the epistle to the Ephesians as follows: " Christ also loved the church, and gave himself for it; that he might sanctify and cleanse it with the washing of water by the word ;"† that is, by the *words* used in the form of *baptism*, as St. Chrysostom interprets.‡ If then *baptism* is the ordinary instrument whereby Christ *cleanses* the members of his church; by the same he must be supposed to *justify* them; as *cleansing* and *justifying* are words of like import, in this case, meaning the same with *remission of sins*, which is one great part of *justification*.

St. Paul elsewhere speaks of his new converts, as " putting off the body of the sins of the flesh by Christian circumcision," that is, baptism, "buried with Christ in baptism, and risen with him through the faith of the operation of God,—having all their trespasses forgiven them."§ What is this but saying, that they were *justified*, instrumentally, by *baptism?* The same thing is, at the same time, said to be

---

* Gal. iii. 26, 27.

† Ephes. v. 25, 26. Significatur heic omnino Baptismus, verbo junctus, tanquam *instrumentum* purificationis. *Wolfius* in loc. Compare Pearson on the Creed, art. x.

‡ Chrysostom in loc. tom. xi. p. 145. item Damascen. in loc. Op. tom. ii. p. 190.

§ Coloss. ii. 11, 12, 13. See Wolfius in loc. Wall's Hist. of Infant Bapt. part i. c. 2. Defence, p. 269, &c. Blackwall, Sacr. Classics, tom. ii. p. 189.

brought about by *faith*,* (which is indeed the instrument of *reception* on man's part, as *baptism* is of conveyance on God's part,) but still that very *faith* is supposed to be exerted in, and completed by, *baptism*, before it *justifies*, so far as it does *justify*.

I proceed to a noted text in the epistle to Titus: " Not by works of righteousness which we have done, but according to his mercy he saved us, by the washing of regeneration, and renewing of the Holy Ghost ;—that being justified by his grace, we should be made heirs according to the hope of eternal life."† It is manifest, by comparing the three verses together, that *baptism* is here made the mean through which, or the instrument by which, the *Holy Spirit* of God worketh *regeneration, renovation*, and *justification;* and that *justification*, the last named, is, in order of nature, (though not in order of *time*,) the last of the three, as the result of the two former, in the same work of grace, in the same federal solemnity. It may be noted by the way, that *baptism*, in this text, is not considered as a work of man, but as an *instrument, rite*, or *federal transaction* between *God and man*.

In the epistle to the Hebrews, we read thus: "And having a high priest over the house of God, let us draw near with a true heart in full assurance of faith, having our hearts sprinkled from an evil conscience, and our bodies washed with pure water. Let us hold fast the profession of our faith,"‡ &c. In these few words are pointed out the *meritorious cause* of our *justification*, expressed by the sprinkling, viz. with the *blood* of Christ, in allusion to the *blood* of ancient *sacrifices;* the *instrumental mean* of conveyance, *baptism*, expressed by the washing of our bodies ; and the instrumental mean of reception, expressed by the word *faith*. The *merits* of Christ, applied in *baptism* by the spirit, and received by a lively *faith*, complete our *justification* for the time being. I know not whether the apostle's here laying so much stress upon our *bodies* being *washed with pure water*

* Διὰ τῆς πιστεως τῆς ἐνεργειας τευ Θεου. Ea infertur *efficacia* et *virtus* Dei, quæ *fidem* in Colossensibus procrearit, similis illi, qua Christum excitavit ex mortuis. *Wolf*. in loc.

† Tit. iii. 5, 6, 7. Compare Regeneration Stated, upon this text. De Baptismo hæc accipienda esse Patres crediderunt:—nec aliter interpretes recentiores tantum non omnes. *Wolfius* ad loc.

‡ Heb. x. 21, 22, 23.

might not, among several other similar considerations drawn from the New Testament, lead the early fathers into a thought which they had, and which has not been so commonly observed; namely, that the application of *water* in *baptism* secured, as it were, or sealed the *body* to a happy *resurrection:* while the spirit more immediately secured the *soul;* and so the *whole man* was understood to be spiritually *cleansed,* and *accepted* of God, in and by *baptism.** They had also the like thought with respect to the *elements* of the *other* sacrament, as appointed by God for *insuring* the *body* to a happy *resurrection* along with the *soul.*† Whether that *ancient rational* of the *two sacraments* be not, at least, as good as any *modern* ones, I leave to be considered, and pass on.

St. Peter says, " Baptism doth also now save us; not the putting away of the filth of the flesh, but the answer [stipulation,] of a good conscience towards God, by the resurrection of Jesus Christ."‡ What I have hereupon to observe is, that baptism *saves:* that is, it gives a just *title* to salvation; which is the same as to say, that it conveys *justification.* But then it must be understood not of the *outward washing,* but of the *inward lively faith,* stipulated in it and by it. *Baptism* concurs with *faith,* and *faith* with *baptism,* and the *Holy Spirit* with both; and so the merits of Christ are savingly applied. Faith *alone* will not ordinarily serve in this case; but it must be a *contracting* faith on *man's part,* contracting in form, corresponding to the *federal* promises and engagements on *God's part:* therefore Tertullian rightly styles baptism *obsignatio fidei.*§ *testatio fidei, sponsio salutis,*‖ *fidei*

* The thought is thus expressed by an eminent *father* of the *second* century:

Corpora enim nostra per *lavacrum* illam quæ est ad incorruptionem unitatem acceperunt; *animæ* autem per *Spiritum:* unde et utraque necessaria, cum utraque proficiunt ad vitam Dei, &c. *Irenæus,* lib. i. c. 17. p. 208. edit. Bened. Compare Tertullian de Baptismo, c. iv. p. 225. De Anima, c. xl. p. 294. Cyrill. Hierosol. Catech. iii. p. 41. Nazianzen. Orat. xl. p. 641. Hilarius, Pict. in Matt. p. 660. edit. Bened. Nyssenus, Orat. de Bapt. Christi, p. 369. Cyrill. Alex. in Joann. lib. ii. p. 147. Ammonius in Catena in Joann. p. 89. Damascen. de Fid. Orthodoxa, lib. iv. c. 9. p. 260.

† Irenæus, lib. iv. c. 18. p. 251. lib. v. c. 2. p. 293, 294. Tertullian. de Resur. Carnis. c. viii. p. 330. Cyrill. Hierosol. Mystag. iv. p. 321. Paschasius de Corp. et Sang. Domini, c. xix. p. 1602.

‡ 1 Pet. iii. 21. See my Review, vol. vii. c. xi. p. 318.

§ Tertullian. de Pœnit. c. vi. p. 125. Conf. de Resur. Carn. c. xlviii. p. 355. ‖ Tertullian. de Bapt. c. vi. p. 226.

E 2

*pactio,** and the like. But I shall say more on the head of
faith in a distinct article below.

There is yet another very observable text, which might
have come in, in its place; but I chose to reserve it to the
last, for the winding up this *summary view* of the *Scripture
doctrine* on this head. It runs thus: "Such were some of
you: but ye were washed," (*viz.* in *baptism,*) "but ye were
sanctified, but ye were justified in the name of the Lord
Jesus, and by the spirit of our God."† I think it better to
render it *were,* or *have been,* than *are,* as best suiting with
the *original,* and with the *were,* just going before; but the
sense is much the same either way. Here are *three concur-
rent causes* of *justification* (together with *sanctification,*) mentioned together: *viz.* the *meritorious cause,* the *Lord Jesus;*
the *efficient* and *operating cause, the spirit of our God;* and the
instrumental rite of *conveyance, baptism.* From these several
passages of the New Testament laid together, it sufficiently
appears, not only that *baptism* is the *ordinary instrument* in
God's hands for conferring *justification;* but also, that ordinarily there is no *justification* conferred either *before* it or
without it. Such *grace* as *precedes* baptism amounts not ordinarily to *justification,* strictly so called:‡ such as *follows*
it, owes its force, in a great measure, to the *standing virtue*
of *baptism* once given.§

Secondly. To confirm what has been here proved from
Scripture, or rather to show the more plainly that we are
not mistaken in so interpreting, I may next briefly add the
concurring verdict of the *ancients,* bearing testimony to the
same doctrine, down from St. Barnabas of the first age,
about the year seventy, to the end of the fourth *century,* or
later.

Barnabas declares, that *baptism procures remission of sins;*‖
therefore it procures *justification.* He declares farther, that
men descend into the water *full of sins and pollutions:* there-

* Tertullian. de Pudicit. c. ix. p. 562.
† 1 Cor. vi. 11. See Wolfius in loc. Bull. Op. Lat. p. 411, 422.
‡ Vid. Augustin. de divers. Q. ad Simplic. tom. vi. lib. i. p. 89. item
epist. cxciv. p. 720. and compare Regeneration Stated.
§ Vid. Augustin. de Nupt. et Concupisc. tom. x. lib. i. p. 298. Compare my Review, &c. vol. vii. p. 240, 241.
‖ Το βαπτισμα το φερει εις αφεσιν αμαρτιων. *Barnab. Epist.* c. xi. p.
36. Ημεις μεν καταβαινομεν εις το υδωρ γεμοντες αμαρτιων και ρυπου, και
αναβαινομεν καρποφορουντες κ. τ. λ. *Ibid.* p. 38.

fore, by his account, they are not *justified*, ordinarily, *before* baptism. Some *moderns* have imagined the *ancients* built their *strict notions* of the *use* and *necessity* of baptism upon too rigorous a construction of John iii. 5. But it is certain that they had those strict notions before St. John's Gospel was written; and that Barnabas, in particular, pleaded texts out of the *Old* Testament for the same doctrine, and that *later* fathers had several other texts to produce, besides John iii. 5. such as I have cited. But I proceed.

Hermas, of the same *century*, affirms, that a Christian's *life is and shall be saved by water;*[*] which amounts to the same with what we have before seen in St. Peter, and admits of like interpretation. His elsewhere declaring *remission of sins* to belong to *baptism*,[†] imports as much as saying that *justification* hangs upon it. In another place, he expresses his sense of the *necessity* of *baptism* to *salvation* (consequently to *justification*) still more positively.—"Before any one receives the name of the Son of God, he is liable to *death*: but when he receives that *seal*, he is delivered from *death*, and is assigned to *life*. Now that *seal* is *water*, into which persons go down liable to *death*, but come out of it assigned to life."[‡] Here it is plain, that *baptism* is pre-supposed to *justification*, which is made the *effect* and *consequent* of it. I defend not Hermas's *inference* or *retrospect*, with respect to the ancient patriarchs. *Baptism* is the *gospel instrument* of *justification:* but *other symbols*, and other *instruments*, served the *same purpose* under the *preceding dispensations*.[§]

Justin, of the next age, undertaking to describe the *order* and *method* of training up, and admitting *new converts* to Christianity, particularly observes, that they who are per-

[*] Quoniam vita vestra *per aquam* salva facta est et fiet: fundata est enim verbo omnipotentis et honorifici nominis. *Herm.* lib. i. vis. 3. sect. 3. p. 798. ed. Fabric. Compare Wall's Hist. of Inf. Bapt. part. i. cap. 1. p. 2.

[†] In aquam descendimus, et accipimus remissionem peccatorum nostrorum. *Herm. Mandat.* iv. sect. 3. p. 854.

[‡] Antequam enim accipiat homo nomen filii Dei, *morti* destinatus est: at ubi accipit illud *sigillum*, liberatur a *morte*, et traditur *vitæ.* Illud autem sigillum *aqua* est, in quam descendunt homines *morti* alligati, ascendunt vero *vitæ* assignati. *Herm. Sim.* ix. sect. 16. p. 1008. Compare Wall, part i. cap. 1. p. 2—5. and Bingham xi. 4, 6. p. 203, 204.

[§] Vid. Augustin. Enchirid. p. 241. tom. vi.

suaded, and *do believe* those things to be *true* which are
taught them, and do undertake to *live* accordingly, are directed to fast and pray for the *forgiveness of their former
sins ;* and are afterwards brought where there is *water*, and
so they are *regenerated*, being *washed with water*, in the
name of the *three divine persons ;* (the necessity of which is
apparent from John iii. 3, 4, 5, and Isaiah i. 16, 20.) and
then they receive remission of sins *in water;* but provided
that they truly *repent* them of their sins.* The *order* here
specified runs thus : *faith, repentance, baptism, dedication* to
God, *renovation* in Christ, *remission of sins*, which is *justification*. The *two* first *preceded* baptism ; the *three* last accompanied it, as the *fruits* and *effects* of it, being *subsequent*
in order of *casuality*, if not in order of *time*. Preparatory
grace, we know, must be *before all :* but Justin had no occasion there to be particular on that head.

Irenæus, thirty or forty years later in the same century,
teaches, that every son of Adam needs the *laver of regeneration* to relieve him from the *transgression* with which he
is born;[†] that is, to *save* him, as he elsewhere explains.[‡]

Clemens, of the same time, speaking of *baptism*, says:
" Being *baptized* we are *illuminated*, being *illuminated* we
are made *sons*, being made *sons* we are *perfected*, being *perfected* we are *immortalized.*—This work is variously deno-
minated ; *grace*, and *illumination*, and *perfection*, and *laver :
laver*, by which we wipe off sins ; *grace*, by which the pe-
nalties due to sins are remitted ; *illumination*, by which that
holy and salutary light is viewed, that is, by which we gaze
on the Divine Being."§   *Baptism* is here supposed to be

* Justin Mart. Apol. i. p. 88, 89, 90. edit. Lond. Compare Wall.
Inf. Bapt. part i. cap 2. p. 12, 13. 2d edit.
† Quoniam in illa plasmatione, quæ secundum *Adam*, fuit, in *trans-
gressione* factus homo indigebat *lavacro regenerationis;* postquam linivit
lutum super oculos ejus, dixit ei, *vade in Siloam, et lavare;* simul et
plasmationem, et eam quæ est per lavacrum *regenerationem* restituens
ei.   *Iren.* lib. v. cap. xv. p. 312. edit. Bened.
‡ Omnes enim venit per semetipsum *salvare:* omnes, inquam, qui
per eum *renascuntur* in Deum, infantes, et parvulos, et pueros, et ju-
venes, et seniores.   *Iren.* lib. ii. cap. 22. p. 147.
§ Βαπτιζομενοι, φωτιζομεθα· φωτιζομενοι, υικτοιουμεθα· υιοτοιωμενοι, τελευομε-
θα· τελευομενοι, απαθανατιζομεθα.—καλειται δι πολλαχως το εργον τουτο,
χαρισμα, και φωτισμα, κ τελειον, και λουτρον· λουτρον μεν, δι ου τας αμαρτιας
απορρυπτομεθα· χαρισμα δι, ω τα ετι τοις αμαρτημασιν επιτιμια ανιται·
φωτισμα δι, δι' ου το αγιον εκεινο φως το σωτηριον εποπτευεται, τουτιστιν δι' ω

the *instrument* of *illumination, remission, adoption, perfec-tion, salvation:* under which, jointly considered, must be comprehended all that concerns *justification*, though the *name* itself is not used.

Tertullian calls *baptism* " the happy sacrament of water, whereby we are washed from the *sins* of our former blind-ness, and recovered to eternal life."* He adds that we are *born in water*, and are no otherwise *saved* than by the abid-ing in it by the use of it in baptism.† He answers the ob-jection drawn from the *sufficiency* of *faith alone*, as in the instance of Abraham. The sum of his solution is, that what was not required *formerly* is requuired *now:* that the *gospel* has made a *new law*, a *new rule* for it, and has tied us up to such form. He refers to Matt. xxviii. 19, and to John iii. 5, and to the instance of St. Paul, recorded in the Acts; who, though he had before *faith* sufficient, yet was strictly required to *add baptism* to it.‡ From hence it is plain that Tertullian understood *baptism* to be the ordinary and indispensable *mean* or *instrument* of *justification;* insomuch that he thought even a *layman* guilty of *destroying a soul*, if he should refuse to give a person *baptism* in a case of *extremity*, no *clergy* being present.§ Nevertheless, the same Tertullian indulged some particuliarities as to the point of *delaying* baptism in some cases; and has been thought not very *consistent* with himself in that article; especially where

το Θειον εξυπτουμιν. *Clem. Alex. Pædag.* lib. i. cap. 6. p. 113. edit. Oxon. Conf. Nazianzen. de Bapt. Orat. xl. p. 638.

* Felix sacramentum aquæ nostræ, qua abluti delictis pristinæ cæci-tatis, in vitam æternam liberamur. *Tertullian. de Bapt.* cap. i. p. 224.

† In aqua nascimur: nec aliter quam in aqua permanendo *salvi* sumus. *Ibid.* Præscribitur nemini sine baptismo competere *salutem*, ex illa maxime pronuntiatione Domini, qui ait, *nisi natus ex aqua, &c. Ibid.* cap. xii. p. 228. Conf. de Anima, cap xl. p. 294.

‡ Hic ergo scelestissimi illi provocant quæstiones: adeo dicunt, baptismus non est *necessarius*, quibus *fides* satis est; nam et Abraham nullius aquæ nisi *fidei*, sacramento Deo placuit. Sed in omnibus *poste-riora* concludunt, et *sequentia* antecedentibus prævalent. Fuerit salus per *fidem nudam*, ante domini passionem et resurrectionem. At ubi fides *aucta* est, credendi in nativitatem, passionem, et resurrection-em ejus, addita est *ampliatio* sacramento, obsignatio baptismi, *vestimen-tum* quodammodo fidei, quæ retro erat *nuda*, nec potest [esse] jam sine sua *lege*. Lex enim tinguendi imposita est, et forma præscripta. *Tertull. de Bapt.* cap. xiii. p. 229.

§ Reus erit *perditi hominis*, si supersederit præstare quod libere potuit. Cap. xvii. p. 231.

he makes it an argument for such *delay*, that "faith entire is secure of salvation."* But he hereby only *qualified* his *former doctrine*, so as to *except* some very *rare* and *extraordinary* cases, where delays might be made, not out of *contempt*, but *reverence* towards the sacrament: otherwise the *ordinary* rule was to stand inviolable.† As to the *excepted* cases, they would be *rare* indeed, since *baptism* might be had upon very short warning‡ in any *extremity* almost according to *his* principles, if so much as a *laic* could but be found to confer it. But I return to the point in hand.

Cyprian, more cautious in the point of *delays* than his master Tertullian, gives this reason why the *baptism* of *infants* should not be deferred (in danger of death) to the *eighth* day; that it is our duty, so far as in us lies, to take care that *no soul be destroyed*.§ It is plain from hence, that he thought there was ordinarily, no *justification* previous to *baptism*, the *appointed channel* of *conveyance*, the fountain head of the spiritual life: for such was Cyprian's opinion of it, as appears through all his writings.‖ Not only so, but he expressly mentions *justifiation* as one of the graces conferred in it.¶

I pass on to the next century; where we find the *elder* Cyril declaring, that a person comes to *baptism bearing his sins, dead in sins*, (therefore not yet *justified*.) but that he comes out *quickened in righteousness*;'* which is the same as to say, *justified*.

* Si qui pondus intelligant baptismi, magis timebunt *consecutionem* quam *dilationem:* fides integra secura est de salute. Cap. xviii. p. 232.
† See Wall, Hist. of Inf. Bapt. part i. cap. 4. p. 23. Bingham, xi. 4. 10. p. 212.
‡ Cæterum omnis dies domini est, omnis hora, omne tempus habile baptismo, cap. xix. p. 233.
§ Universi judicavimus, nulli homini nato misericordiam Dei et gratiam denegandam: nam cum Dominus in evangelico suo dicat, *Filius hominis non venit animas hominum perdere,* sed *salvare;* quantum in nobis est, si fieri potest, nulla anima perdenda est. *Cyprian. Epist.* lix. ad Fidum, p. 98. edit. Bened.
‖ Cyprian. Epist. i. p. 2. Epist. xxiii. p. 32. Epist. lxxii. p. 128. Epist. lxxiv. p. 140. Epist. lxxvi. p. 155, 157. De Habit. Virgin. p. 180. Testimon. lib. iii. cap. xxv. p. 314. De Orat. Domin. p. 206.
¶ Quomodo tales *justificare* et *sanctificare* baptizatos possunt, qui hostes sacerdotum, &c. *Epist.* lxxvi. p. 155.
** Κατερχη μεν γαρ υς το υδωρ φεραι τας αμαρτιας· αλλ' η της χαριτος στιχλησις σφραγισατα την ψυχην, εν συη χαρη λωπει υπο του φοβου καταποθηναι δρακοντος.

Basil, of the same century, expresses himself fully to our purpose, in these words; " Whence are we Christians? By *faith*, will every one say. But after what manner are we *saved?* By being *regenerated* through the *grace* which is conferred in *baptism.*—For if *baptism* is to me the *beginning* of life, and that *regeneration day* is the *first* of days; then it is manifest that voice is of all the most *precious* which is sounded forth upon the *grace of adoption.*"* *Baptism* is here supposed to be, as it were, the *first delivery* of *God's grant* of *adoption,* * and consequently of *justification,* which is much the same thing. *Faith* goes before, as the *hand* stretched out, ready to *receive:* but it cannot be received before it is *given:* neither is it ordinarily first *given,* but in *baptism;* nor *continued* afterwards but in *virtue* of it, *due qualifications supposed* all the while. In another chapter the same father says, " *Faith* and *baptism* are two means of salvation, near akin to each other, and *inseparable.* For *faith* is *perfected* by *baptism,* and *baptism* is *grounded* in *faith,* and both are *completed* by the same [divine] names."†

Hilarius Diaconus, some years before Basil, taught the same doctrine; interpreting St. Paul's quotation from the Psalmist (which the Apostle applies to the purpose of *justification,* Rom. iv. 6, 7, 8.) of what is done in *baptism,* of the *justification conferred* in that *holy solemnity :*‡ from whence

νεκρος εν αμαρτιαις καταβας, αναβαινεις ζωοποιηθεις εν δικαιοσυνη.   *Cyril. Hierosol.* Catech. iii. p. 45. edit. Bened. Conf. Catech. xvii. p. 282.

* Χριστιανοι ποθεν ημεις; δια της πιστεως πας τις αν ειποι σωζομεθα δε, τινα τροπον; Αναγεννηθεντες, δηλονοτι, δια της εν τω βαπτισματι χαριτος.——ει γαρ αρχη μοι ζωης το βαπτισμα, και πρωτη ημερων εκεινη η της παλιγγενεσιας ημερα, δηλον οτι και φωνη τιμιωτατη πασων η εν τη χαριτι της υιοθεσιας εκφωνηθεισα. *Basil. de Spirit. Sanct.* cap. x. p. 21, 22. edit. Bened.

† Πιστις δε και βαπτισμα, δυο τροποι της σωτηριας, συμφυεις αλληλοις, και αδιαιρετοι, πιστις μεν γαρ τελειουται δια βαπτισματος· βαπτισμα δε θεμελιουται δια της πιστεως, και δια των αυτων ονοματων εκατερα πληρουνται. *Basil. ibid.* cap. xii. p. 23.

‡ Propheta autem tempus felix prævidens in Salvatoris adventu, *beatos* nuncupat, quibus sine labore vel aliquo opere *per lavacrum* remittuntur, et teguntur, et non imputantur, peccata. Apostolus tamen propter plenitudinem temporum, et quia plus gratiæ in *Apostolis* est quam fuit in *Prophetis,* majora prostestatur quæ ex *dono baptismatis* consequimur; quia non solum *remissionem peccatorum* accipere nos, sed *justificari* et *filios Dei* fieri profitetur, ut *beatitudo* hæc perfectam habeat et securitatem et gloriam. *Hilar. Diac. in Rom.* iv. 8. inter. Opp. Ambros. tom. ii. p. 49.

it is evident that he understood *baptism* to be the *ordinary standing mean, or instrument of conveyance.*

I shall shut up this detail of *fathers* with the words of St. Austin; who, undertaking to explain the *four things* mentioned by the Apostle, (Rom. viii. 30.) *predestinate, called, justified,* and *glorified,* says of the *third* thus: " Behold, persons are *baptized,* all their sins are forgiven, they are *justified* from their sins."* He repeats the same doctrine soon after in words still more express.† It would be endless to quote passages from the same father to prove that, in his account, there is no *justification, before* or *without baptism.* It was a fixed principle with him, that *justification* ordinarily *commenced* with *baptism,* and not *otherwise.*

From hence (as I may note by the way) we may easily understand what St. Austin meant by his *famed maxim,* which many have often perverted to a very wrong sense; namely, that *good works follow after justification, and do not precede it.*‡ In reality, he meant no more than that men must be *incorporated in* Christ, must be Christians, and *good Christians,* (for such only are *justified,)* before they could practise *Christian works,* or *righteousness,* strictly so called:§ for *such works only* have an *eminent right* and *title* to the name of *good works;* as *they only* are *salutary* within the *covenant,* and have a *claim* upon *promise.* Works before

---

* Ecce enim *baptizati* sunt homines, omnia illis peccata dimissa sunt, *justificati* sunt a peccatis. *Augustin.* Serm. clviii. de verb. Apostol. Rom. viii. 762. tom. v.

† Unusquisque vestrum jam ipsa *justificatione* constitutus, accepta scilicet remissione peccatorum *per lavacrum regenerationis,* accepto Spiritu Sancto, proficiens de die in diem, &c. *Augustin. ibid.* p. 763. Conf. Chrysostom. in Rom. vii. 30. Hom. xv. p. 595. tom. ix. ed. Bened. Damascen. in eund. loc. Opp. tom. ii. p. 33.

‡ Sciat se quisque per *fidem* posse justificari, etiamsi *legis* opera non præcesserint: *sequuntur enim justificatum non præcedunt justificandum. Augustin. de Fid. et Oper.* cap. xiv. p. 177. tom. vi. Justificationem opera non præcedunt. *Augustin. de Spirit. et Litera,* cap. xxvi. p. 109. tom. x. Bona opera subsequuntur gratiam, non præcedunt. *Opp. imperf. contr. Julian.* lib. i. cap. 141. p. 956. tom. x. Conf. tom. ii. p. 717, 720, et tom. vi. p. 89.

§ Mandata ejus sancta et bona sibi tribuebant; quæ ut *possit* homo facere, Deus operatur in homine per fidem Jesu Christi qui finis est *ad justitiam* omni *credenti :* id est, cui per Spiritum *incorporatus,* factusque *membrum* ejus potest quisque, illo incrementum intrinsecus dante, *operari justitiam. Augustin. de Spiritu. et Lit.* cap. xxix. p. 113. Conf. cap. xxxiv. p. 119. tom. vi.

justification, that is, before salutary *baptism,* are not, in his account,[*] *within* the *promise;* but are *excluded* rather, according to the *ordinary* rule laid down in John iii. 5. and diverse other texts before cited. But I return.

Enough hath been said to show that *baptism* is, by divine appointment, the *ordinary instrument* for conveying the grace of *justification. Scripture* and *antiquity* are clear in this matter: and so likewise are our *church forms;* particularly our *baptismal*[†] offices, *catechism,* and *confirmation.*

I am aware that some eminent *moderns*[‡] have presumed to teach, that the *first* justification in adults is *antecedent* to baptism, and that *baptism* rather *seals* and *confirms* it, than *conveys* it: but I see no sufficient ground for that doctrine, either in *scripture* or *antiquity,* or in the *public offices* of our **church**; but much the contrary: and it seems, that the mistake in this matter first arose, either from the confounding the first prepartory *renewings* of the grace of the spirit, with the grace of *justification ;* or from a misinterpreting of St. Paul's doctrine relating to *justifying faith,* as if the apostle in mentioning *one* instrument of justification, had thereby excluded every instrument *besides,* which he does not. It might as well be pleaded (as I before hinted,) that the apostle had thereby excluded the work of the *Father,* or *Son,* or *Spirit,* from the office of *justification;* as that he excluded the visible *means, rites,* or *sacraments,* in and by which they jointly operate. St. Paul's phrases, or *exclusive terms,* infer no such thing; neither is his *faith* opposed to *baptism,* but it takes it in, ordinarily, and is neither *salutary* nor *lively* faith, till *plighted in that ordinance.*[§]

[*] Vid. Augustin. de divers. Quæst. ad Simplic. lib. i. p. 18. tom. vi. Item de Spirit. et Lit. cap. xxxiv. p. 119. tom. vi.

[†] Publ. Bapt. of Inf. and Private Bapt. and Bapt. of those of riper years. [‡] Bucer. Script. Anglican. p. 730.

[§] This article was maintained, against Cartwright, by Whitgift first, and afterwards by Hooker. (See Hooker, vol. ii. b. 5. n. 60. p. 245. Ox. edit.) Field, after both, vindicates the Protestants on that head against the reproaches of their Popish adversaries, as follows:

"Stapleton saith, that a threefold fraud of the Protestants, touching remission of sins, is to be avoided: first, in that they make our *justification* to consist in the *sole* remission of sins by *faith,* that the *sacraments* confer nothing to our *justification.* But this is untrue; for they teach no such thing; but that *baptism* and *repentance* are necessarily required in them that are to be *first* justified." *Field on the Church,* b. iii. Append. p. 298.

F

5. From the instrument of *conveyance* on *God's part*, we may next proceed to the instrument of *reception* on *man's;* which I take to be *faith*, as I have more than once intimated, and must now explain.

I am sensible that some very eminent men[*] have expressed a dislike of the *phrase* of the *instrumentality* of *faith;* and have also justly rejected the *thing*, according to the *false* notion which some had conceived of it. It cannot, with any tolerable sense or propriety, be looked upon as an instrument of *conveyance* in the hand of the *efficient* or *principal* cause: but it may justly and properly be looked upon as the instrument of *reception* in the hand of the *recipient*. It is not the *mean* by which the grace is *wrought, effected,* or *conferred:* but it may be, and is, the *mean* by which it is *accepted* or *received :*[†] or, to express it a little differently, it is not the *instrument* of justification in the *active* sense of the word; but it is in the *passive* sense of it.

It cannot be for nothing that St. Paul so often and so emphatically speaks of man's being justified *by faith*,[†] or through *faith* in Christ's blood ;[§] and that he particularly notes it of Abraham, that he *believed*, and that his *faith* was *counted* to him for *justification;*[||] when he might as easily have said, had he so meant, that man is justified by *faith and works*, or that Abraham, to whom the *gospel* was *preached*,[¶] was justified by *gospel faith* and *obedience*. Besides, it is certain, and is on all hands allowed, that, though St. Paul did not directly and expressly oppose *faith* to *evangelical works*, yet he comprehended the works of the *moral law*

---

[*] Hammond, Catech, Opp. vol. i. p. 36. Tillotson, Posth. Serm. vol. ii. p. 480, 486. Bull. Opp. Latin. p. 418, 512, 555, 655, 657, 658. Truman, Great Propit. p. 194, 195.

[†] Quod per fidem, tanquam *organum*, gratiam justificationis *accipi* vel *apprehendi* dicunt Protestantes, næ illi Romanenses——nimium *morosi* censores sunt, quibus ista loquendi forma improbatur; præsertim propter verbum *apprehendendi:* eodem enim modo loquuntur etiam multi doctissimi Romanenses. *Pererius in Rom.* v. 2. Maldonat. in Joh. vi. 29. videatur, et Estius in Rom. iii. 28. Claudius Espencæus in 1 Tim. vi. 12. ubi horum novorum criticorum temeritatem recte castigat. Gul. Forbes, Consid. Modest. p. 24. Conf. p. 38. edit. nova, A. D. 1704.

[‡] Rom. i. 17. iii. 22, 28, 30. v. 2. ix. 32. Gal. ii. 16. iii. 8, 11, 14, 22, 24, 26. v. 5. Phil. iii. 10.

[§] Rom. iii. 25. Gal. ii. 20. Phil. iii. 10.   [||] Rom. iv. 3. Gal. iii. 6.

[¶] Gal. iii. 8.

under those works which he excluded from the *office of justifying*, in his sense of *justifying*, in those passages: and farther, he used such arguments, as appear to extend to *all kinds* of *works:* for Abraham's works were really *evangelical* works, and yet they were *excluded.* Add to this, that if *justification* could come even by *evangelical works*, without taking in *faith* in the meritorious sufferings and satisfaction of a mediator; then might we have " whereof to glory,"[*] as needing no pardon ; and then might it be justly said that " Christ died in vain."[†] I must further own, that it is of great weight with me, that so early and so considerable a writer as Clemens of Rome, an apostolical man, should so interpret the doctrine of *justifying faith*, as to *oppose* it plainly even to *evangelical* works however exalted. It runs thus : " They (the ancient patriarchs) were all therefore greatly glorified and magnified; not for their own sake, or for their *own works*, or for the *righteousness* which they themselves wrought, but through his good pleasure. And we also being called through his good pleasure in Christ Jesus, are not *justified* by ourselves, neither by our own wisdom, or knowledge, or *piety*, or the *works* which we have done in *holiness of heart*, but by *that faith* by which Almighty God *justified* all from the beginning."[‡] Here it is observable, that the word *faith* does not stand for the whole system of Christianity, or for *Christian belief* at large, but for some particular *self-denying* principle by which good men even under the *patriarchal* and *legal* dispensations, laid hold on the *mercy* and *promises* of God, referring all, not to *themselves* or their *own deservings*, but to *divine goodness* in and through a *mediator*. It is true, Clemens elsewhere, and St. Paul almost every where, insists upon true *holiness of heart* and *obedience of life*, as indispensable *conditions* of salvation or *justification;* and of that, one would think there could be no question among men of any judgment or probity : but the question about *conditions* is very distinct from the other question about *instruments;* and therefore both parts may be true, viz. that *faith* and *obedience* are *equally conditions,*

---

* See Rom. iv. 2.   † See Gal. ii. 21.

‡ Και ημεις ουν δια θελημα τος αυτου εν Χριστω 'Ιησου κληθεντες, ου δι' εαυτου δικαιουμεθα, ουδε δια της ημετερας σοφιας, η συνεσιας, η ευσεβιας, η εργων ων κατηργασαμεθα εν οσιοτητι καρδιας· αλλα δια της πιστιας, δι' ης παντας τους απ' αιωνος ο παντοκρατωρ Θεος εδικαιωσεν. *Clem. Rom. Epist.* i. cap. 32.

and *equally indispensable* where *opportunities* permit; and yet *faith* over and above is emphatically the *instrument* both of *receiving* and *holding* justification, or a title to salvation.*

To explain this matter more distinctly, let it be remembered, that God may be considered (as I before noted) either as a party *contracting* with man on very *gracious* terms,† or as a *judge* to *pronounce judgment* upon him.

Man's first coming into covenant (supposing him *adult*) is by *assenting* to it, and *accepting* of it, to have and to hold it on such *kind of tenure* as God *proposes*: that is to say, upon a *self-denying tenure*, considering himself as a *guilty* man, standing in *need* of *pardon*, and of *borrowed* merits, and at length resting upon *mercy*.‡ So here the *previous* question is, whether a person shall *consent* to hold a privilege upon this *submissive* kind of tenure or not? Such *assent* or *consent*, if he comes into it, is the *very thing* which St. Paul and St. Clemens call *faith*:§ and this *previous* and

* A learned foreigner illustrates this matter by the case of *marriage*, as every good person is conceived to be married to Christ, and to become one flesh with him. Ephes. v. 31, 32. Now there are many *qualifications, conditions, capacities*, requisite to a *valid* marriage: but still *consent* or *contract*, with due solemnities, is what formally *makes* the matrimonial bond, and what gives it its sanction. Respect, obedience, love, do not properly *effect* it; but *consent* does. So *faith* binds the contract, consummates the marriage covenant with Christ, while the rest are considered as *qualifications* or *conditions* of the stipulation, not as the formal stipulation itself. *Vid. Wesselii Dissertat. Academ.* p. 147, &c. 281.

† Neque enim hoc *fœdus* naturam habet *emptionis, venditionis*, aut *locationis, conductionis*, aut alicujus contractus *innominati, do ut facias, facio ut facias*, ubi eorum quæ invicem præstantur *æqualitas* requiritur: sed habet aliquam convenientiam cum contractu *feudali*, ubi uni pars *ex gratia* quid in alterum confert, quæ autem altera vicissim præstat, non *retributionis* sed tantum *recognitionis* vim habent, grati, fidelis, ac devoti animi testem. *Puffendorf. Jus Fecial. Divin.* sect. liv. p. 191. Conf. sect. li. p. 172.

‡ Summa hoc redit, quod is [Christus] peccata generis humani, in se suscepit, eaque, expiavit, ac pro iisdem justitiæ Divinæ satisfecit, eo cum effectu ut qui in ipsum *credunt*, seu in ejusdem *merito* et *satisfactione* omnem suam *fiduciam* reponunt, *ejus intuitu* gratiam Dei quærunt, peccatorum remissionem, *solidam* et coram tribunali divino subsistentem *justitiam*, cum aliis beneficiis quæ cum Deo reconciliatos comitantur, et demum *vitam æternam* consequantur. *Puffendorf. ibid.* sect. xlviii. p. 166.

§ Quia fœdus ac Divina beneficia per eandem [fidem] *acceptantur;*

general question, is the question which both of them deter-
mine against any *proud claimants* who would hold by a more
self-admiring tenure.

Or, if we next consider God as sitting in judgment, and
man before the tribunal, going to plead his cause; here the
question is, what *kind* of *plea* shall a man resolve to trust
his salvation upon? Shall he stand upon his *innocence*,
and rest upon *strict law*; or shall he plead *guilty*, and rest
in an *act of grace?* If he chooses the *former*, he is proud,
and sure to be *cast:* if he chooses the *latter*, he is *safe* so
far, in throwing himself upon an *act of grace.* Now this
question also, which St. Paul has decided, is *previous* to the
question, what *conditions* even the act of grace itself finally
insists upon? A question which St. James in particular,
and the *general* tenor of the whole Scripture has abundantly satisfied ; and which could never have been made a *question* by any considerate or impartial Christian. But of that
I may say more under another article. What I am at present concerned with is to observe, that *faith* is emphatically
the *instrument* by which an adult *accepts* the covenant of
grace, *consenting* to hold by *that kind* of *tenure*, to be *justified* in *that way*, and to rest in *that kind* of *plea*, putting his
salvation on *that* only issue.

It appears to be a just observation, which Dr. Whitby
makes, (Pref. to the Epist. to Galat. p. 300) that Abraham
had *faith* (Hebr. xi. 8.) before what was said of his *justification* in Gen. xv. 16. and afterwards more abundantly,
when he offered up his son Isaac: but yet neither of those
instances was pitched upon by the apostle, as fit for his
purpose, because in both *obedience* was joined with *faith:*
whereas here was a pure *act of faith* without *works*, and of
this *act of faith* it is said, " it was imputed to him for righteousness."

The sum is, none of our *works* are good enough to stand
by *themselves* before him who is of *purer* eyes than to behold
iniquity. Christ only is *pure* enough for it at first hand,
and they that are Christ's at second hand, in and through

cum invitis et reluctantibus ista impingere nolit Deus, neque id citra
extinctionem *moralitatis* fieri possit. *Ibid.* sect. li. p. 172. Ex parte
hominum ordinavit medium λπτικ:ν, seu per quod istud acceptatur,
fidem; quam etiam hominibus offert, sed *morali*, non *physico* aut *me-
chanico* modo. *Ibid.* sect. lxxviii. p. 319. Conf. sect. lxxxv. p. 349.

him.   Now, because it is by *faith* that we thus interpose,
as it were Christ between *God* and *us*, in order to gain *acceptance* by him ; therefore *faith* is emphatically the *instrument* whereby we *receive* the grant of *justification*.   *Obedience* is equally a *condition*, or *qualification*, but not an *instrument*, not being that *act* of the *mind* whereby we *look up*
to God and Christ, and whereby we *embrace* the promises.
   "Faith," by St. Paul's account of it, "is the substance
of things hoped for," as making the things *subsist*, as it were,
with certain effect in the mind.   It is the "evidence of
things not seen,"* being, as it were, the eye of the mind,
looking to the *blood* of Christ, and thereby inwardly warm-
ing the affections to a firm reliance upon it and acquiescence
in it.†   But this is to be understood of a *firm* and *vigorous*
faith, and at the same time *well grounded.*—*Faith* is said to
embrace (salute, welcome,) the things *promised* of God,‡ as
things *present* to view, or near at hand.   There is no other
faculty, virtue, act, or exercise of the mind, which so properly does it as *faith* does : therefore *faith* particularly is
represented as that by which the Gentile converts *laid hold
on* justification,§ and brought it home to themselves.   And
as *faith* is said to have *healed* several,‖ in a *bodily* sense ;
so may it be also said to *heal* men in a *spiritual* way, that
is, to *justify*, being immediately *instrumental* in the *reception*
of that grace more than any other *virtues* are.   For as, when
persons were *healed* by *looking on* the *brazen serpent*,¶ their
eyes were particularly *instrumental* to their *cure*, more than
the *whole body;* so *faith* the *eye* of the mind, is particularly
instrumental in this affair, more than the *whole body* of graces
with which it is accompanied : not for any supereminent
excellency of *faith* above every other virtue, (for *charity* is
greater**) but for its particular *aptness*, in the very *nature* of
it, to make things *distant* become *near*, and to admit them
into close embraces.   The Homilies of our Church describe
and limit the doctrine thus : "*Faith* doth not shut out *repentance*, *hope*, *love*, *dread*, and the *fear* of God, to be *joined*

---

* Hebr. xi. 1.   † Rom. iii. 25.   ‡ Hebr. xi. 13, 14.
§ Rom. ix. 30, 31, 32.

‖ Matt. ix. 22. Luke vii. 50. viii. 48. xvii. 19. xviii. 42. Mark, v. 34.
x. 52.

¶ Numb. xxi. 8, 9.   Comp. Isa. xlv. 22.   John iii. 14.   Conf. Gul.
Forbes, Confid. Modest. p. 28, 29.   Grabe in Notis ad Bulli Harmon.
p. 450, 451.   ** 1 Cor. xiii. 13.

OF THE DOCTRINE OF JUSTIFICATION.

with *faith* in every man that is *justified;* but it shutteth them out from the *office* of justifying;"* that is to say, from the *office* of *accepting* or *receiving* it: for as to the *office* of *justifying* in the *active* sense, *that* belongs to God *only,* as the same homily elsewhere declares.† The doctrine is there further explained thus: "Because *faith* doth directly *send us* to Christ *for remission of our sins,* and that, by *faith* given us of God, we *embrace* the *promise* of God's mercy, and of the remission of our sins, (which thing none *other* of our *virtues* or *works* properly doth,) therefore the Scripture useth to say, that faith *without works* doth *justify:*"‡ not that this is to be understood of a man's being confident of his *own* election, his *own* justification, or his *own* salvation in particular, (which is quite another question, and to be determined by other rules,) but of his *confiding* solely upon the *covenant of grace* in Christ, (not upon his *own deservings,*) with full assurance that so and *so only,* he is *safe* as long as he behaves accordingly.

The *covenant of grace* has *conditions* annexed to it, which I am next to consider.

ⅰ 6. The *conditions* of *justification* are of great weight; for

* Homily of Salvation, part i. p. 19.

† Homily of salvation, part ii. p. 22, 23. and part iii. p. 24. Among the *later* Homilies, see on the Passion, p. 347, 349. and concerning the Sacrament, part i. p. 376, 379. Conf. Norwelli Catech. p. 41. Gul. Forbes, Consid. Modest. p. 23, 24, 38. Hooker, Disc. on Justific. p. 509. Tyndal. p. 45, 187, 225, 330, 331. Field, p. 298, 323. Conf. Augustan. art. xx. p. 18, 19. Spanheim, tom. iii. p. 141, 159, 761, 834. Le Blanc, p. 126, 267.

‡ Homily of Salvation, part iii. p. 24.

N. B. In the 28th Article of our Church, we are taught that "*the mean* whereby the body of Christ is *received* and eaten in the supper, is *faith.*" Compare Jewell's Defence, &c. p. 234. and my Review, vol. vii. p. 104, 105, 144, 156, 177, 179, 394. No one can doubt but that *charity* is as necessarily required to a *worthy* reception of the *Eucharist,* or to a *real* reception of the *body* and the *graces* thereon depending, as *faith* can be: they are *both* of them *equally conditions:* but *faith* particularly is the *mean,* or *instrument;* which *charity* in this case is not. *Charity* is excluded here from serving as a *mean,* from the *office* of being an *instrument;* and nobody takes offence at it; why should they therefore in the other *sacrament,* the sacrament of the *first* justification, when the cases are parallel? Our Church is constant and uniform in *both;* and so are the *ancient* churches likewise, upon reasons grounded in the very nature of *faith,* as an act or habit *specifically different* from *charity.*

without them no *instruments* can avail. Those *conditions* are
faith and *obedience ;* as St. James hath particularly maintained.*   St. Paul had before determined the *general* and *pre-*
vious question, as to the *tenure* whereby we are to hold, or
the *plea* by which we ought to abide; namely by *grace,* in
opposition to *claims :* and when some *libertines* had perverted
(as is probable) St. Paul's doctrine very widely and strange-
ly, and made an ill use of it; then St. James showed that
that very *faith,* which was to rest in a covenant of *grace,*
supposed a *conformity* to the *terms* of it; otherwise it would
be found but a *dead faith,* no *Christian faith* at all; for a
cordial belief of the divine *promises,* and a *cordial acquiescence*
in God's *covenant, implies* and *includes* a *cordial submission*
to the *terms* and *conditions* of it; otherwise it is nothing but
empty *ceremony.*

Upon the whole, the perfect agreement between St. Paul
and St James, in the article of *justification,* appears very
clear and certain. St. Paul declares, that, in order to come
at *justification,* it is necessary to stand upon *grace,* not upon
merit; which St. James does not *deny,* but *confirms* rather in
what he says of the *perfect law* of *liberty,* James i. 25. ii. 12.
St. Paul makes *faith* the *instrument* of *receiving* that grace;
which St. James does not dispute, but *approves* by what he
says of Abraham, (chap. ii. 23.) only he maintains *also,* that
in the *conditionate* sense, *justification* depends *equally* upon
faith and *good works;* which St. Paul also *teaches* and *incul-*
cates in effect, or in other words, through all his writings.
If St. Paul had had precisely the *same* *question* before him
which St. James happened to have, he would have decided
just as St. James did: and if St. James had had precisely
the *same question* before him which St. Paul had, he would
have determined just as St. Paul did. Their *principles* were
exactly the *same,* but the *questions* were *diverse,* and they had
different *adversaries* to deal with, and opposite *extremes* to
encounter, which is a common case.

It may be noted, that that *faith* which I here call a *con-*
dition, is of much wider compass than that *particular* kind
of faith which is precisely the *instrument of justification.* For
faith, as a *condition,* means the *whole complex* of *Christian be-*
lief as expressed in the *creeds;* while *faith,* as an *instrument,*
means only the laying hold on *grace,* and resting in Christ's

* James ii. 14—26.

merits in opposition to our *own deservings:* though this also, if it is a *vital* and *operative* principle, (and if it is not, it is nothing worth,) must of course *presuppose*, carry with it, and draw after it, an hearty *submission* to, and *observance* of all the necessary *conditions* of that *covenant* of *grace*, wherein we repose our whole trust and confidence. So that St. Paul might well say, " Do we then make void the law (the moral law) through faith? God forbid : yea we establish the law."*
We exempt no man from religious *duties;* which are *duties* still, though they do not *merit*, nor are practicable to such a degree as to be above the need of *pardon:* they are necessary *conditions*, in their measure of *justification;* though not *sufficient* in themselves to *justify*, nor *perfect* enough to stand before God, or to abide trial : therefore Christ's *merits* must be taken in to *supply* their defects; and so our resting in Christ's *atonement*, by an humble, self-denying *faith*, is our last resort, our anchor of salvation both sure and steadfast, after we have otherwise done our utmost towards the fulfilling of God's sacred laws, towards the performing all the *conditions* required.†

That *good works*, *internal* and *external*, are, according as *opportunities* offer and *circumstances* permit, ~~conditions~~ properly so called, is clear from the whole tenor of Scripture, as hath been often and abundantly proved by our own *divines*,‡ and is admitted by the most judicious among the *foreign reformed*.§

* Rom. iii. 31.   See Norris's Pract. Disc. vol. iii. Disc. 3.

† Coram Deo nihil valet quam *Filius* ejus charissimus, Jesus Christus: ad illum ubicunque est, respicit; in illo complacuit: hic *totus* sanctus et purus est coram illo.   Filius autem non per *opera*, sed per *fidem* in corde absque omni opere, *apprehenditur*. Charitas et opera nec sunt nec esse possunt Filius Dei, aut *justitia* quæ coram Deo *pura* et sancta sit, ut est *Filius*. Itaque per se non consistunt coram Deo ut *justitia pura*, qualis est *Filius*. Quod vero *justa* et *sancta* vocentur, ex *gratia* fit, non ex *jure:* neque illa æque raspicit Deus ut *Filium*, sed tantum propter *Filium* ea tolerat, et fert illorum impuritatem: imo *coronat* ea et præmiis afficit, sed id omne propter Filium, qui in corde habitat per *fidem*. *Luther. in Seckendorf.* lib. iii. p. 357. A. D. 1541.

‡ Bull. Opp. Latin. p. 412, 414, 415, 430, 434, 514, 516, 544, 583, 645, 668, edit. ult.
Stillingfleet's Works, vol. iii. p. 367, 380, 393, 398.   Tillotson's Posth. Serm. vol. ii. p. 484, 487.

§ Vossius de Bonis Operibus, Thes. x. p. 370. Opp. tom. vi. Frid. Spanhem. fil. Opp. tom. iii. p. 141, 159. Conf. Gul. Forbes, Consid. Modest. p. 195, &c.

Yet some have been very scrupulous as to this innocent name, even while they allow the *absolute necessity* of good *works*, as indispensable *qualifications* for future blessedness. Why not *conditions* therefore, as well as *qualifications?* Perhaps, because that name might appear to strike an *absolute* predestination, or *unconditional* election ; and there may lie the scruple : otherwise, the difference appears to lie rather in *words* than in *things*.

Some will have them called not *conditions*, but *fruits* or *consequents* of justification. If they mean by *justification*, the same as the *grace* of the Holy Spirit, and the *first* grace of *faith* springing from it, they say true :* and then there is nothing more in it than an *improper* use of the word *justification*, excepting that from *abuse* of *words* very frequently arises some corruption of *doctrine*.

If they mean only, that *outward* acts of righteousness are *fruits* of *inward* habits or dispositions ; that also is undoubtedly true : but that is no reason why *internal* acts, virtues, graces, (*good works* of the *mind*,) should not be called *conditions* of the *primary* justification ; or why the *outward* acts should not be justly thought *conditions* of *preserving* it.

But if they mean that *justification* is ordinarily given to *adults*, without any preparative or previous *conditions* of *faith* and *repentance*, that indeed is very *new* doctrine and *dangerous*, and opens a wide door to *carnal security* and to all *ungodliness*. But enough of this matter.

The sum of what has been offered under the present head is that we are *justified* by God the *Father*, considered as *principal* and *first mover ;* and by God the *Son*; as *meritorious* purchaser ; and by God the *Holy Ghost*, as immediate *efficient :*

* Nemo computet bona opera *ante* fidem; ubi *fides* non erat, *bonum opus* non erat: bonum enim opus *intentio* facit, intentionem *fides* dirigit. *Augustin. in Psal.* xxxi, p. 172. tom. iv.

Crede in *e*um qui justificat impium, ut possint et bona opera tua esse *opera bona:* nam nec *bona* illa appellaverim, quamdiu non de *radice bona* procedunt. *Ibid.* p. 174.

N. B. St. Austin is not constant in his notion of *good works*, but he uses the phrase in a twofold sense, *larger* or *stricter*. Sometimes he means by *good works*, works flowing from *grace* and *faith*, whether before or after baptism; as he does here: and sometimes he means works strictly Christian, subsequent to the *incorporation* in baptism, that is, subsequent to *justification*. The want of observing this, his twofold use of the phrase has led some uncautious readers into mistakes.

and by *baptism*, as the ordinary *instrument* of *conveyance;* and by *faith* of such a kind, as the ordinary *instrument* of *reception;* and *lastly*, by *faith* and *holiness*, as the necessary *qualifications* and *conditions* in adults, both for the first *receiving* and for the perpetual *preserving* it.* Such and so many are the *concurring causes*, operating, in their order and degree towards man's *first* or *final justification.* It would be altogether wrong to *separate* them, or to set them *one against another*, or to *advance* any one or *more*, to the *exclusion* of the *rest.*

* The order of *justification* is thus expressed in King Edward's catechism, written by Poynet, A. D. 1553, countenanced by the other Bishops and Clergy, and published by the King's authority.

"1. The *first* and *principal*, and most proper cause of our *justification* and *salvation*, is the goodness and love of God, whereby he chose us before the world.

"2. After that, God granteth us to be *called* by the preaching of the Gospel of *Jesus Christ*; when the *Spirit* of the Lord is poured upon us by whose guiding and governance we be led to settle our *trust* in God, and *hope* for the performance of his promise.

"3. With this *choice* is joined, as companion, the *mortifying* of the *old man*, that is of our affections and lusts.

"4. From the same *Spirit* also cometh our *sanctification*, the *love of God* and of our *neighbour;* justice and uprightness of life.

"5. *Finally*, to say all in sum, whatever is in us, or may be done of us, honest, pure, true, and good; that altogether springeth out of this pleasant rock, the goodness, love, choice, and unchangeable purpose of God; he is the *cause;* the rest are the *fruits* and *effects.*

"6. Yet are also the *choice* and *Spirit* of God and *Christ* himself *causes* conjoined and coupled with each other: which may be reckoned amongst the *principal causes* of salvation.

"7. As of therefore as we use to say, that we are *made righteous* and *saved* by *faith only*, it is meant thereby, that *faith*, or rather *trust alone* doth *lay hard upon*,* understand, and perceive our *righteous-making*, to be given us of God *freely;* that is to say, by no *deserts* of our own, but by the *free grace* of the Almighty Father.

"8. Moreover *faith* doth ingender in us *love* of our neighbour, and such *works* as God is pleased withal: for if it be a *lively* and *true* faith, quickened by the Holy Ghost, she is the mother of all good saying and doing. By this short tale, it is evident by what means we attain to be righteous. For, not by the *worthiness* of our own deservings were we heretofore *chosen*, or long ago *saved*, but by the *only mercy* of God, and *pure grace* of Christ our Lord; whereby we were in him made to *do* those *good works* that God had appointed for us to walk in. And although *good works* cannot *deserve* to make us righteous before God, yet do they so *cleave* unto *faith*, that neither *faith* can be found *without* them, nor *good works* be any where found *without* faith." Fol. 68. *in Heylin Quinquartic. contr.* p. 105.

* For *hold.*

I may observe further, for the preventing any mistake or misconception, that I might have considered *baptism* as an *external instrument* of *reception* in the hand of *man*, as man bears a part in that sacrament; and so there would be *two* instruments of *reception*, external and internal, *baptism* and *faith:* and if any one chooses so to state the case, I shall not object to it. But having mentioned *baptism* before, as the *instrument* of *conveyance* on *God's* part, which is most considerable, I thought it of less moment to bring it up again under a different view, because that would be understood of course.

I cannot dismiss this head without throwing in a word or two of the wise provisions made by our church, in bringing *children* to *baptism*, that they may be *regenerated* and *justified* from the first. It is right and safe for the children themselves: and not only so; but the very doing it is further of use to prevent or remove the perplexities raised by contentious men on the subject of *justification*.

Some will tell you that *good works* are not *conditions* of justification: it is certainly true in the case of *infants*, (which is the common case with us,) for neither *works* nor *faith* are *conditions* required of *them:* they are *justified* without either, by the *free mercy* of God through the alone *merits* of Christ.

Some will plead, that man is utterly *unable* to do *good works* before he is *justified* and *regenerated:* they should rather say, before he receives *grace;* for that is the real and the full truth. But what occasion or need is there, for disturbing common Christians at all with points of this nature now? Are we not all of us, or nearly all, (ten thousand to one) *baptized* in *infancy;* and therefore *regenerated* and *justified* of course, and thereby prepared for *good works*, as soon as capable of them by our years? *Good works* must, in this case at least, (which is *our* case) *follow* after *justification* and *regeneration*, if they are at all; and therefore how impertinent and frivolous is it, if not hurtful rather, to amuse the ignorant with such notions, which, in our circumstances, may much better be spared? Our church has so well provided for that case by *infant baptism*, that we need not so much as inquire whether good works *precede* or *follow* justification in the case of *adults*, since it is not our case. We are very sure that, in *our* circumstances, *good works* do not *precede*, but *follow* justification; because they come after *baptism*, if they come at all.   The truth, and the whole truth of this matter seems to lie in the following particulars.

1. *Infants* are *justified* in *baptism*, without either *faith* or *works;* and if they *grow up* in *faith* and *obedience*, the privilege is *continued* to them : if not, it is *taken away* from them, till they *repent*.

2. *Adults*, coming *fitly prepared*, are immediately *justified* in *baptism*, by *faith*, without any *outward* works, without a *good life*, while they *have not time* for it ; but if a *good life* does not *ensue afterwards*, when *time* and *opportunities are given*, they *forfeit* the privilege received, till they *repent*.

3. *Adults*, coming to baptism in *hypocrisy* or *impenitency*, (like Simon Magus.) are not *justified*, whatever their *faith* be ; because they want the necessary and essential *qualifications* or *conditions:* but if they afterwards turn to God with *true faith* and *repentance*, then they enter into a *justified* state, and so continue all along, unless they relapse.

4. Neither *faith* nor *works* are required in *infants:* both *faith* and *inward works* (a change of heart) are required in *all* adults : *faith* and *works* (*inward* and *outward*) are indispensably required in all *adults* who *survive* their baptism, in proportion to their *opportunities, capacities,* or *abilities.* But enough of this.

V.

Having hitherto endeavoured to explain the *nature*, and to set forth the *causes* and *instruments of justification*, in as clear a manner as I could, I proceed now, *lastly,* to point out some *extremes,* which many have been found to run into, on the right hand or on the left: so hard a thing is it to observe a middle course, and to pursue the safe and even road. Those *extremes* or *deviations* are many, but are reducible to two; one of which, for distinction sake, I may call the *proud extreme,* as disdaining to accept the *grace* of *God,* or the *merits* of *Christ;* the other may be called the *libertine extreme,* as abusing the doctrines of *grace* and *satisfaction,* to serve the ends of *licentiousness.*

1. I shall begin with the *proud extreme.* The Pagans formerly, were so proud of their *good morals,* that they conceived they had no need of Christ, either to make them better, or

to secure the divine acceptance; and therefore they would
not so much as listen to the terms of Christianity.*

The Pharisaical Jews were as proud, or prouder, in their
way, claiming, as it were, *justification* as a *debt*,† rather than
a *favour*, as if they had no need of *grace*, or were too exalted
to accept of *pardon*. This high conceit of themselves and
their own perfections, made them averse to Christ, and kept
them from submitting to the *gospel way* of *justification* or *salvation.*

The Pelagians, of the fifth century, by over-magnifying
free will and *natural* abilities, at the same time depreciating
or slighting *divine grace*, unwarily fell into the *proud extreme;*
though not so grievously as the Jews and Pagans had done
before. St. Austin, however, very justly made use of the
same way of reasoning against *them*, which St. Paul had
made use of against Jews and Pagans; because the same
general reasons concluded equally against *all.*‡

The Schoolmen of later days, and the Romanists still
later, one by setting up a kind of *merit* of *congruity*§ as to
works preceding justification, and the other by maintaining
a *merit* of *condignity*‖ with respect to works following, and

* Multi enim gloriantur de *operibus*, et invenis multos Paganos prop-
terea nolle fieri Christianos, quia quasi sufficiunt sibi de *bona vita* sua.
Bene vivere opus est, ait; Quid mihi præcepturus est Christus? Ut
bene vivam? jam bene vivo: quid mihi necessarius est Christus? Nullum *homicidium*, nullum *furtum*, nullam *rapinam* facio, res alienas non
concupisco, nullo *adulterio* contaminor: nam inveniatur aliquid in *vita*
mea quod *reprehendatur*, et qui *reprehenderit*, faciat Christianum. *Augustin. in Psal.* xxx. Enarr. 2. p. 171. tom. iv.

† Rom. iv. 4. xi. 6. Compare Truman, Great Propitiation, p. 184,
300.

‡ Hoc possumus dicere quod de lege dicit Apostolus, si *per naturam*
justitia, ergo *Christus gratis mortuus est.*——Qui suis *meritis* præmia
tamquam *debita* expectant, nec ipsa merita Dei *gratiæ* tribuunt, sed
viribus propriæ *voluntatis*, sicut dictum est de carnali *Israel, persequentes
legem justitiæ, in legem justitiæ non perveniunt. Quare? Quia non ex
fide, sed tamquam ex operibus.* Rom. ix. 31. 32. Ipsa est enim justitia
ex fide, quam Gentes apprehenderunt, de quibus dictum est. Rom. ix.
30.——Ipsa est justitia ex fide, qua credimus nos *justificari*, hoc est,
justos fieri, gratia Dei per Jesum Christum Dominum nostrum.——
Quæ ex Deo justitia in fide, in *fide* utique est, qua credimus nobis justitiam *Divinitus* dari, non *a nobis*, in *nobis*, *nostris viribus* fieri. *Augustin. Paulino Epist.* clxxxvi. p. 664, 666. tom. ii.

§ Against Merit of Congruity, see the 13th Article of our Church.

‖ Concil. Trident Sess. vi. Can. 32. Bellarmin. de Justificat. lib. v.
cap. 17.

by admitting *works* of *supererogation*,* have apparently run too far into the *proud extreme;* only differently modified, or under a *form*, somewhat different from that of the self-assuming claimants of older times. Wherefore the first *reformers*, finding that the same *general* reasons, which St. Paul had made use of in another case, might be justly applicable in this case also; they laid hold of them, and urged them with irresistible force against all kinds of human *merit*, or pretended *merit*, however disguised, or however set off with art or subtilty. Thus came the doctrine of justification by *faith alone*,† that is to say, by the *alone merits* and *cross* of *Christ*, (as Bishop Jewell interprets it,‡) to be a distinguishing principle of the *reformation*.

The Socinians, by rejecting *Christ's satisfaction*, and of course standing upon their own works as available to salvation, independent of it, have only chosen another way of committing the same fault, and of running into the *proud extreme*.

The Deists, who boast of their *morality*,§ in opposition to *gospel faith* and *gospel obedience*, are, in this respect, so nearly allied to the *pagan philosophers*, who lived in Christian times, that they may be said to fall under the same predicament with them; excepting only the additional aggravation of their *apostacy* from the faith whereunto they had been baptized.

Those *enthusiasts*, who fear not to boast even of a *sinless perfection* in this life; they (whatever their pretences are) are remarkably peccant in the *proud extreme*, even to a degree of *madness*, and stand condemned by many express passages both of Old Testament and New.

Lastly, If there be any amongst us, as probably there

* Against which, see the 14th Article of our Church.
† See the 11th Article of our Church.
‡ Jewell, Def. of Apology, p. 66.
§ Their main principle is thus expressed in a Latin distich:
Haud crucient animum quæ circa religionem
Vexantur lites; sit modo vita proba.   *Baro. Herbert.*
See my Discourse on Fundamentals, vol. viii. p. 121, 122, 123.

Near akin to these, are such as magnify moral virtues, pagan virtues, as acceptable in themselves, and needing no *atonement* nor *sacrament* to recommend them to the Divine acceptance. See the Nature, Obligation, and Efficacy of the Christian Sacraments, vol. v. p. 472, 473, 478. and Supplement, p. 526, 527, &c. 535, 536, 537.

may, who, though knowing themselves to be *sinners*, yet think that the *good works* of *alms*, or other the like bounden duties, will satisfy for their *sins;* and who thereupon conceive that God would do them *wrong*, if he should not, for their *good* deeds, *pardon* their *evil* deeds ; such also may be said to err in the *proud extreme*, not considering that all their *good deeds* are only so many *strict dues*, and that the paying off a debt *in part*, entitles no man to a *discharge* for the *remainder.* God, for Christ's sake,* may give a discharge for the *whole* to every *penitent* offender, after his sincerely performing *some part* of his duty : but a man's own *good works*, be they ever so many or so great, cannot *in themselves* be pleaded by way of proper *atonement* for his sins.

Having thus briefly enumerated the most, or the most common mistakes or miscarriages in the matter of *justification*, on the *assuming* side, derogating from the honour of God's *free grace*, and from the *merits* of Christ, which are the valuable *considerations* upon which, or for the sake of which only, God justifies as many as he does justify ; I shall now proceed to observe something of the common *mistakes* in the *other extreme*, which concerns the necessary, essential *conditions* or *qualifications* required in every *adult* whom God shall accept.

2. It is a dangerous and fatal *extreme* so to magnify, or

* Non patitur enim *justum* Dei judicium, ut *justum* censeat aliquem qui *justitiam* non habeat: non habet vero *justitiam* ullam *peccator* nisi in *Christo*, et per mysticam arctissimamque illam *unionem* cum Christo. Jer. xxiii. 6. 2 Cor. v. 21. 1 Cor. i. 30. Quæque ideo tantopere inculcatur in N. T. ubi fideles sexcentis in locis dicuntur esse *in Christo*. Et celebratur pariter in V. T. in Psal. xlv. Cantico Canticorum toto. Isa. liv. 5. Hos. ii. 18, 19. Quia scilicet *in ea* est fundamentum *justificationis* peccatoris coram Deo. Vinculum vero hujus *unionis* præcipuum, absque quo *unio* hæc nullatenus consistit, est *fides* actualis in Christum, moriturum olim, nunc mortuum, in adultis; vel *Spiritus fidei* in infantibus electis. *Wesselius. Dissert. Academ.* p. 148. Tum tandem *justificari* peccatorem coram Deo *sola fide*, qua *dextram* dat sponso ac sponsori, ejusque *dextram* tenet, et qua sola *conhubium stabile* cum ipso contrahens, *justitia vicaria* ejus imputatur illi ut *sua*, et jus accipit ad omnia ejus bona.——Bona opera postea imponuntur justificatæ (reginæ) ut in quibus non est *causa* regnandi, sed *via* tantum ad regnum gloriæ. Omnes ergo externe *vocati* (quibus *Rex* Messias sponsor fœderis, cum *justitia vicaria*, omnique *gratia* ejus quotidie offertur in Evangelio, quibusque ipse *dextram suam conjugalem* blande porrigit) semetipsos diligenter et serio examinare debent, num huic *reginæ*, seu *Ecclesiæ* veræ, ut ejus *membra* genuina, accenseri queant. *Ibid.* p. 281.

to pretend to magnify *grace* or *faith*, as thereby to *exclude*, *sink*, or any way *lessen* the *necessity* of true and sincere, and (so far as human infirmities permit) universal *obedience*.[*] There is the greater need of the utmost caution and circumspection in this particular, because corrupt nature is very prone to listen to, and to fall in with any appearing arguments, any pretexts, colours, handles for *relaxation of duty*, and for *reconciling* their *hopes* and their *lusts* together. St. Paul was aware, that some of ill minds might be apt to pervert his sound doctrine of *justification* by *faith*, to the purposes of *licentiousness;* but *truth* was not to be suppressed for fear some should *abuse* it; (for what is there which some or other may not make an ill use of?) neither would it have been right to let *one extreme go uncorrected*, only for the preventing the possible, or even probable danger from weak or evil-minded men, who might take the handle to run into *another*. St. Paul therefore was content so to correct an error on the right hand, as, at the same time, to guard against a greater on the left.[†]

Notwithstanding all his *guards*, some there were, (as he supposed there would be,) who, even in the *apostolical age*, did *pervert* the doctrine of *grace*, to serve the ends of *licentiousness:* and some or other, probably, have done the like, designedly or undesignedly, in every age since. St. Paul had taught, that none of our works are *pure* or *perfect* enough to abide the *divine scrutiny*, or to *claim* justification as a debt,[‡] or a matter of *right;* which is undoubtedly true: but *libertines* changed that *true* and *sound* proposition into this very *unsound* one ; that *good works* are not so much as necessary *conditions* or *qualifications* for *justification*. St. Paul had also taught that *faith* or an humble *reliance* upon the *grace*

---

[*] *Signa* fidei justificantis sunt 1. *Totum* velle Christum suum esse, non tantum ut *sacerdotem*, sed etiam ut *regem*. 2. *Solum* velle Christum, cum abnegatione *justitiæ propriæ*, omniumque *sanctorum*, quæ nulla est. 3. *Gaudere* in *fide*, et animosa in adversis *fiducia* stare ac dextram regis, eique adhærere, etiam dum ducit per ignes et aquas. 4. *Abnegare* voluntatem *propriam* quandoque *naturalem*, semper *pravam* ac *perversam*, et regis *voluntati* arcanæ et ravelatæ se patienter ac prompte submittere. Si horum nihil in semetipsis deprehendant, hoc ipso momento, absque ulla dilatione, *fide sincera* fœdus *conjugale* contrahant, &c.——Si vero horum aliquid in se ipsis inveniant gratias immortales agant——*Stent* porro in fide animosi, &c. p. 281, 982.

[†] See Rom. iii. 31. vi. 1, &c.   [‡] Rom. iv. 4. xi. 6.

of God through the *merits* of Christ, in opposition to self-boasting,* or standing upon the *perfection* of *our own performances*, was our only *safe plea* before God, our only *sure way* to be *justified*, after doing the best we could for performing our bounden duties: this *true* and *important* proposition some turned into quite another, *contradictory* to the whole tenor of the *gospel;* viz. that faith alone, a dead faith, separate from evangelical *obedience*, is the *only condition* of salvation. Against such *dogmatizers*, and against such loose principles, St. James engaged, reproving and confuting the men and their errors in few, but very strong words.† St. Peter also and St. John, though more obscurely, combated the same errors.‡

That some or other, in after ages, were very prone to run into the extreme of *licentiousness*, taking an handle from the doctrine of *grace;* as others were apt to run into the *proud extreme*, from the doctrine of the value and necessity of a *good life;* may be judged from what a *father* of the fifth century says in opposition to both.§

It is certain that the Antinomian and Solifidian doctrines, as taught by some in later times, have deviated into a *wild extreme*, and have done infinite mischief to *practical Christianity.* I have not room to enumerate, much less to confute, the many erroneous and *dangerous tenets*, which have come from that quarter: neither would I be forward to expose them again to public view. They have been often *considered* and often *confuted*. Let them rather be buried in oblivion, and never rise up again to bring reproach upon the *Christian name*. But take we due care so to maintain the doctrine of *faith*, as not to *exclude* the *necessity* of *good works;* and so to maintain *good works*, as not to *exclude* the *necessity*

* Rom. iii. 27. 1 Cor. i. 29, 31.   Ephes. ii. 9.   Rom. iv. 2.
† James ii. 14—26.   ‡ 2 Pet. i. 5—10. 1 John iii. 7—10.
§ Si se homo justificaverit, et de *justitia sua* præsumserit, *cadit:* si considerans et cogitans infirmitatem suam, et præsumens de *misericordia Dei*, neglexerit vitam sum mundare a peccatis suis, et se omni gurgite flagitiorum demerserit, et *ipse cadit.* Præsumptio de justitia quasi *dextera* est: cogitatio de impunitate peccatorum, quasi *sinistra* est. Audiamus vocem Dei dicentem nobis, *ne declines in dexteram aut sinistram.* Prov. iv. 27. Ne præsumas ad regnum *de justitia tua:* ne præsumas peccandum de misericordia Dei. Ab utroque te revocat præceptum divinum, et de illa *altitudine*, et ab ista *profunditate:* illuc si ascenderis, præcipitaberis: hac si lapsus fueris, demergeris. *Augustin. in Psal.* xxxi. p. 171. tom. iv.

of Christ's *atonement*, or the *free grace* of God. Take we care to perform all evangelical duties to the utmost of our power, aided by God's spirit; and when we have so done, say, that we are *unprofitable servants,* having no strict *claim* to a reward, but yet looking for one, and accepting it as a *favour,* not challenging it as *due* in any right of our *own*; due only upon *free promise,* and that promise made not in consideration of any *deserts* of *ours,* but in and through the alone *merits,* active and passive, of Christ Jesus our Lord.